100 DESI STORIES
TO
INSPIRE YOU

100 DESI STORIES

TO
INSPIRE YOU

Madhur Zakir Hallegua

JAICO PUBLISHING HOUSE

Ahmedabad Bangalore Bhopal Bhubaneswar Chennai
Delhi Hyderabad Kolkata Lucknow Mumbai

Published by Jaico Publishing House
A-2 Jash Chambers, 7-A Sir Phirozshah Mehta Road
Fort, Mumbai - 400 001
jaicopub@jaicobooks.com
www.jaicobooks.com

© Jaico Publishing House

100 DESI STORIES TO INSPIRE YOU
ISBN 978-81-8495-766-2

First Jaico Impression: 2015
Third Jaico Impression: 2016

Page design and layout: SÜRYA, New Delhi

Printed by
Nutech Print Services-India
B-25/3, Okhla Industrial Area, Phase-II
New Delhi - 110 020

Contents

CONFIDENCE *and* STRESS MANAGEMENT

CREATIVITY
and
INNOVATION

1

Think Creatively

Vikram was well-known in the village for his creativity and problem-solving skills. Many people approached him to show them the way out of their seemingly unsolvable problems.

Once, his young friend came to him crying. On asking him what had happened, his friend said, 'I was very hungry, but all I had with me was one chapati. I had nothing to eat it with. I was standing outside a hotel when the delicious aroma of a spicy dish caught my attention. Having nothing to do, I sat below a tree and ate my chapati.

But the owner of the hotel came out and caught hold of me. He said, 'You have eaten your chapati while enjoying the aroma of the food from my hotel. Now you must pay me for the dish you were enjoying.'

I protested that since I hadn't eaten the dish, there was no reason for me to pay for it. Yet, he shouted at me and asked me to go home and get the money to pay him. Neither have I eaten his dish, nor do I have the money to pay him. Please help me!'

'Let's go and meet the hotel owner,' said Vikram to his friend. Though his friend was very reluctant, he trusted Vikram's judgement and went with him to meet the hotel owner. 'My friend has come to pay you for the dish that he has not consumed,' said Vikram. 'I have been waiting for your friend,' said the hotel owner.

Then the creative Vikram brought out his wallet and took out some coins. The hotel owner put out his hand to accept the money. But neither did Vikram pay the owner, nor was the owner able to protest against Vikram's settlement.

Think Tank

1. How did Vikram settle the problem?

2. What can you learn from this story?

The Think Tank encourages you to answer these questions on your own before referring to the answers given below.

Answers

1. Vikram took out some coins from his wallet, but did not hand them over to the hotel owner. Instead, he kept the coins in one hand, placed the other hand over it and shook his hands so that the sound of the coins could be heard. When the owner asked what was going on, he replied that as his friend had eaten his chapati accompanied only by the aroma of the food, it was only fair that he pay the hotel owner with the sound of the coins.

2. A difficult problem can be easily solved with the use of creativity. Where most of us get stumped, a creative thinker can easily find a solution to overcome an apparently difficult problem. Through his creativity, Vikram found the apt solution and solved his friend's problem.

2

The Mantra for Household Peace

Radha was a worried woman. She was fed up with the young generation in general and her daughter-in-law in particular. 'That young chit of a girl has no respect for her elders. Why can't she follow my orders while doing the housework? She wants to do everything as per her wish. How I wish I hadn't agreed to this marriage!' she told her neighbour.

When Ramesh came back from work, he took one look at his mother's face and knew that yet another argument had taken place that day. How he wished his mother would back off! His wife Yamini was good at housework, though she favoured the latest gadgets while cooking. But one had to adopt the prevalent trends, he thought.

His mother Radha had been married young and was widowed while Ramesh was still a child. With the responsibilities of earning an income and looking after her in-laws and Ramesh, Radha had grown old before her time. When Ramesh got married, she had looked forward to some peace. But now, she looked more worried than ever.

'Tomorrow you must come with me to Panditji,' she told him. 'And please, not a word to that wife of yours!' Ramesh did not believe in astrologers. Of course, Panditji was a very learned and respected astrologer in the village.

The next morning, Ramesh and Radha went to meet Panditji. Radha told him all about Yamini and how she was suffering from her behaviour. 'Please give me a solution, Panditji. Anything to get away from this torture!' Ramesh looked sceptical. How was an astrologer supposed to solve domestic problems? He found Panditji watching him keenly.

Panditji consulted his charts. 'Hmm,' he said. 'The planets are showing some malefic effects. Your problem is serious. It can go away but you will have to strictly follow what I say.' Radha nodded.

He said, 'I will give you a mantra. You must chant it for two hours in the morning and two hours in the evening, for it to work. The mantra is:

Shri Ram Jai Ram Jai Jai Ram

It is a wonderful mantra for household peace. You must do this lifelong. Only then can your problem be solved.' As Radha murmured assent, Ramesh once more thought about how this was going to work.

But Radha was determined to give it a try. She religiously chanted the mantra for two hours every morning and evening. Gradually, Ramesh noticed that there were now lesser arguments between Yamini and his mother. They were civil to each other nowadays and his mother also looked at peace. Perhaps, it was really the power of the mantra, he thought. After another month of peace, he was convinced. I must apologize to Panditji. I didn't believe his mantra would work, he thought with remorse.

The next morning found him at Panditji's house. Panditji welcomed him and asked him how his domestic problem was. 'Completely solved, Panditji. Now they are not only civil but even at peace with each other. Your mantra for peace in the house has worked wonders. I can't thank you enough!' said Ramesh.

To his surprise, Panditji laughed out loud. 'Of course, the mantra is a powerful one, my friend. It has the power to solve many problems in the world. But it is not meant for household peace!'

'Then how did it work?' asked Ramesh surprised.

Think Tank

1. If the mantra was not for household peace, how had the problem been solved?

The Think Tank encourages you to answer the question on your own before referring to the answer given below.

Answer

1. Though the mantra was a powerful one, it was actually not the mantra that had worked. Panditji was a practical man who clearly understood that the problem was Radha. He had told Radha to chant the mantra for two hours each morning and evening. This would keep her busy and out of Yamini's way. Yamini would be able to do the housework in peace. After two hours of chanting the mantra, Radha would be in no mood to fight with Yamini or look into the household chores. This ensured that there was no interference and peace prevailed.

3

'My' God!

Five-year-old Richa had come to stay with her grandmother for the holidays. Her grandmother was a drawing teacher. She wanted Richa to develop a liking for art during these vacations.

Richa began to learn to draw with her grandmother's help. After about 15 days of drawing all sorts of shapes, one day her granny asked her, 'Richa, what would you like to draw today?' Richa thought for a while and said, 'Today, I will draw God!'

Her granny was taken aback. She wondered how Richa was going to draw God. But she decided not to discourage the child. Richa drew for about ten minutes.

Her granny was waiting with excitement. She was hoping Richa would become a fine artist someday. She was eager to see what Richa had drawn.

Though she was doubtful that Richa would be able to draw the idol from their homes, she certainly hoped she would be somewhere close.

'I'm done, granny. Come, see my drawing,' said Richa. Granny came to see what Richa had drawn. She was shocked, amazed and disappointed to see that Richa had drawn circles, squares and zigzag lines all over the page.

'What's this, Richa?' asked granny disappointed.

'God,' answered Richa.

'This drawing is not correct, Richa. This is not God. Haven't you seen God whom we pray to in our temples and in our homes? You must draw Him. Come, I will teach you to draw Him.'

Richa looked at her granny for one full minute and told her, 'Granny, He is *your* God. What I have drawn is *my* God!'

Think Tank

1. What is the moral of the story?

The Think Tank encourages you to answer the question on your own before referring to the answer given below.

Answer

1. As we know, God can be described or drawn in a number of ways. A child is innocent and ready to believe that God exists in the squares, circles and zigzag lines that she has drawn. Unlike us, there are no specifications or rather limitations of shape, size and colour in her mind.

4

The Vessel Full of Milk

Facing persecution, when the Parsi community first came to India, they arrived at Sanjan which is in Gujarat. They requested the king, Jadi Rana to grant them asylum so that the community could settle down in Gujarat.

However, the king was not very eager to have them settle there. He sent them a vessel filled with milk up to the brim to signify that his kingdom was full and there was no place for them in his kingdom.

In response, the Parsi leader added some sugar to the milk.

The king was impressed and gave the community permission to settle down in Gujarat.

Think Tank

1. What did the Parsi leader want to communicate through his action?

The Think Tank encourages you to answer the question on your own before referring to the answer given below.

Answer

1. The king sent the vessel full of milk to indicate that there was no space to accommodate the Parsi community. The leader added sugar to indicate that just as adding sugar does not add to the volume of the milk, rather, it increases its sweetness, they too would only add sweetness to the lives of the citizens of the kingdom.

5

The Right Answer

There was once a pompous king. He was very interested in astrology. He had an astrologer at court who would advise him daily. He had also issued an invitation to all astrologers who were passing through his kingdom to visit him and offer consultations. He would then reward them.

Many astrologers from far and wide came to offer him their consultation and he listened to all of them. In the hopes of getting many rewards, they all told him positive things like how he was a blessed man, how his subjects were pleased with him and how he would have a wonderful crop that year etc.

One day, an aged astrologer came to his court. The king welcomed him and asked for a consultation. The poor old astrologer was a straightforward man. When the king asked him how long he would live, the astrologer told him, 'O King! You will have to live a long life all alone. Your relatives and friends will all die before you and so will your queen. You will be left alone.'

The pompous king was extremely enraged on hearing this. What! Left all alone without his relatives, friends and queen! Impossible!

He straightaway declared that the astrologer be imprisoned for such a prediction. However, this didn't help him at all. The astrologer's prediction depressed him no end and nothing could put him out of his misery. This went on for many days.

Then his minister said to him, 'O King! Do not be so disheartened. Why don't you ask our court astrologer if the old astrologer's prediction is even true in the first place? After all, he has never made any such prediction till date.' The king was somewhat relieved on hearing this and told him to present the court astrologer. The minister told the astrologer the whole story.

The astrologer opened his books, did his calculations and said, 'O King! That astrologer knows nothing! Had there been something of the sort, no doubt I would have told you about it long ago. My prediction is...'

The pompous king smiled a few moments later.

Think Tank

1. What was the court astrologer's prediction?

2. Why did it make the king happy?

The Think Tank encourages you to answer these questions on your own before referring to the answers given below.

Answers

1. The court astrologer said, 'O King! You are the only one among all your relatives who is blessed with a long, healthy life. You will live the longest among them and rule for a very long time to come.'

2. The king was a pompous man. He was not interested in the truth. He only wanted to hear things that were favourable to him. The court astrologer had perfected the art of telling the truth in a way that the king liked to hear. This soothed the king's ruffled feathers and made him happy.

6

The Smart Artist

Long ago, there lived a cruel king who was blind in one eye. Once, he told his minister that he wanted to have a beautiful portrait of his painted. He asked the minister to find him three of the best artists in the kingdom. Of course, each artist was told that if the king liked his portrait, he would be rewarded, but if not, the artist was doomed.

The first artist painted the king's portrait exactly similar to how he was – without one eye. The king was very angry at this contempt by the artist and ordered him to be hanged to death. The second artist painted a beautiful portrait of the king, with both eyes. The king punished him for sycophancy.

Now, it was the turn of the third artist. His painting made the king very happy.

Think Tank

1. How did the third artist paint the king's portrait?

2. What is the moral of the story?

The Think Tank encourages you to answer these questions on your own before referring to the answers given below.

Answers

1. The third artist painted the king's portrait in profile, showing only his good eye.

2. A difficult problem can be solved by using creativity and innovative ideas.

7

Creativity

Mr. Dwivedi was the owner of a company manufacturing Shiny, a well-known brand of soap. Though it was a well-known brand, it was up against stiff competition from multinationals and their products.

As Shiny tried to hold its own in the market, its salesmen began to face a problem with their retailers. Most of its retailers were dealing with multinational brands and paid very little attention to Shiny. They would take its stocks on long-term credit and if the salesmen insisted for payment, they would be told to either take back the stock of Shiny, or would be paid only a part of the due payments. This was resulting into huge amounts of credit for Shiny and was making it difficult for the company to operate.

That's when Mr. Dwivedi came up with two innovative strategies. These strategies not only established Shiny as a leading brand against the multinational companies, but also brought it to a position to dictate terms.

Think Tank
---

1. What were the innovative strategies that Mr. Dwivedi adopted?

The Think Tank encourages you to answer the question on your own before referring to the answer given below.

Answer

1. First, Mr. Dwivedi told Shiny's salespeople to either collect the due payments or take back the stocks of the brand, thus ensuring that no retailer had any stock of Shiny. Once that was done, they ran aggressive media campaigns for an entire month, creating enormous demand. With huge demand and no supply, retailers became desperate to stock Shiny and thus, had to agree to the brand's terms.

8

The Talented Singer

There was a very talented singer called Mandar, at King Digvijay Singh's court. He was known for his melodious voice and his unique style of singing. His fame reached the ears of the king of the neighbouring kingdom, Vishwa Singh. He expressed a desire to hear Mandar sing. King Digvijay Singh immediately invited him to come and hear Mandar.

King Vishwa Singh was welcomed with great festivities. He was given a seat next to King Digvijay Singh on the dais, while Mandar had been given a place at the centre of the court, but which was below the dais.

This angered Mandar who was an arrogant fellow. He refused to take his seat and asked to be seated on the dais, while the kings could sit in his place till the concert got over. King Digvijay Singh was enraged and refused. Mandar lost his temper and walked out of the court in a huff.

King Digvijay Singh was embarrassed at Mandar's behaviour but King Vishwa Singh told him not to worry. King Vishwa Singh had brought along the best singer from his court. He told King Digvijay Singh his idea to get Mandar back to court.

Think Tank
---

1. What was King Vishwa Singh's idea?

2. What is the moral of the story?

The Think Tank encourages you to answer these questions on your own before referring to the answers given below.

Answers

1. King Vishwa Singh asked the singer from his court to sing in Mandar's place. Mandar simply couldn't bear it and came back to the court. He told the kings that the new singer was no good. He would show them what performance was. He then gave the best performance of his life!

2. A person's nature compels him to act in a specific way. Mandar was a singer at heart. King Vishwa Singh knew that he wouldn't be able to bear someone else singing in his place while he looked on, and that he would come back.

9

Filling a Sieve

A professor was talking to his students about creative and innovative thinking. The students said that while they had understood the theory, they wanted to try their hand at a practical problem.

The professor then gave them a sieve. He told them to go to a nearby river and fill the sieve with water. All of them excitedly went to the river bank. However, when they didn't come back for a long time, he went to check what was happening.

He saw that all the students were sitting at the river bank, disappointed. 'It's an impossible task, Sir,' they said. 'We tried all the creative and innovative ideas we could think of, but nothing can fill a sieve with water.'

'Hmm,' said the professor. 'Let me show you,' he said, taking the sieve from them.

Think Tank

1. What did the professor do?

2. What is the moral of this story?

The Think Tank encourages you to answer these questions on your own before referring to the answers given below.

Answers

1. The professor took the sieve and left it in the river water by itself. Soon, it sank. He said, 'Now, your sieve is full of water.'

2. Sometimes we have to keep aside our preconceived notions while solving a problem. The professor hadn't asked the students to bring him the sieve filled with water. They had just assumed so. So, in spite of knowing that the sieve would sink and be filled with water if they just left it in the water, they didn't explore that possibility.

TEAMWORK
and
LEADERSHIP

10

United We Stand,
Divided We Fall

A flock of birds flying in the sky saw some food grains scattered on the ground and swooped down on them. Only after enjoying the grains did they notice that they had landed on a net spread by a hunter and were trapped!

Panicking, each bird made its own meagre efforts to free itself from the net. While some tried to peck at it, others simply tried flapping their wings to get out.

Amid this confusion, a wise old bird in the flock was doing nothing. In frustration, the youngest and the most restless among them asked it why it was not even trying to get out of the net. All the other birds too looked at it in surprise. The wise old bird then told them why.

Think Tank

1. What did the wise old bird say?

2. How did the birds finally get out of the net?

The Think Tank encourages you to answer these questions on your own before referring to the answers given below.

Answers

1. The wise old bird told them that if each of them made individual efforts, they would not succeed, as the size of the net was huge. If they cared only for their own safety, none of them would be able to get free. However, if they all tried together, each one of them would be saved. The problem before them required not individual effort but *teamwork*.

2. The birds accepted the advice of the elderly bird. All of them together lifted the net and flew far away into the jungle. When they landed, the wise old bird called his friend the mouse. The mouse called his friends and they gnawed away at the net and freed the birds.

11

The Strange Condition
of the Feast

This is the story of the *Kauravas* and *Pandavas* from the *Mahabharata*. The *Kauravas* were the hundred sons of the reigning blind king, Dhritarashtra, while the *Pandavas* were the five sons of Pandu (Dhritarashtra's younger brother). The *Pandavas* lived in the forest with their father Pandu, and their mothers, Kunti and Madri. But when Pandu and Madri died, they came back with their mother Kunti, to the palace of their uncle, King Dhritarashtra.

Though they were cousins, the *Pandavas* were often teased and harassed by the *Kaurava* children. The grandfather of the *Pandavas* and *Kauravas* was Bhishma – a learned man as well as an excellent warrior. He tried to ensure that the *Pandava* children were brought up in a fair manner in Dhritarashtra's reign. He also made attempts to foster unity among the *Kauravas* and *Pandavas*.

Once, he asked for a wonderful feast to be organized for the 105 children – 100 *Kauravas* and 5 *Pandavas*. The children were delighted. On the day of the feast, he asked all the children to be seated at their places. After they were served, he announced that they could begin to eat, but there was a rule they had to follow. They had to eat without bending their hands at the elbow.

The children were surprised to hear this. How was it possible? They sat thinking of a solution while the delicious aroma tempted them. Many of the children tried to throw the food in the air and catch it in their mouths but to no avail. Some of them also attempted to lie down on their stomachs and eat the food with their mouths instead of using their hands. But that didn't work either. Finally, they told Bhishma that it was a simply impossible task.

Bhishma then asked Yudhisthir how he would attempt this challenge. Yudhisthir had a solution.

Think Tank

1. What was the solution that Yudhisthir had?

2. Why were the others unable to come up with a solution?

3. What is the moral of this story?

The Think Tank encourages you to answer these questions on your own before referring to the answers given below.

Answers

1. Yudhisthir used teamwork to solve the problem. He picked up a morsel of food and fed it to the eldest *Kaurava* prince, Duryodhan, without bending his hand at the elbow. Yudhisthir said that if they all fed each other, all of them would be able to eat without bending their elbows. All it required was teamwork.

2. Each of the other children thought only about satisfying their

own hunger. Thus, they were unable to come up with any solution.

3. Through teamwork, seemingly impossible problems can also be solved.

12

The Superb Six

The team had lost nine wickets and still had to play the last ten overs. Kabir who had come in to play at number 4 was a good batsman and was still going strong. His partner, Sameer was a great bowler and he had come in at number 10. Everybody was confident that Kabir could score and win the match, but they weren't sure whether the fast-bowling Sameer could survive the last ten overs.

Kabir knew that Sameer had an injury. Though he was trying not to show it, Kabir knew it was difficult for Sameer to play the ten overs. Sameer came up to him and told him, 'Kabir, we must win this match. I am going to give it my all. I am not a great batsman, but I'll support you in every way. Let's go out on all cylinders and win.'

It was just the impetus Kabir needed. He made mincemeat of the bowlers. Sameer was holding up very well. Though he was exhausted, he didn't show it as he thought it might affect his teammate's performance.

It was the last ball of the match. They still needed three runs to win. Kabir knew he just had to hit a boundary!

'Do it one last time, Kabir!' shouted Sameer. As the ball came towards him, a determined Kabir smashed it, and sent it flying way beyond the boundaries for a SIX!

There was a huge uproar, as fans screamed in appreciation. It was truly a brilliant performance! The team had snatched the match from the jaws of defeat!

Their team members came running to the field and lifted Kabir on their shoulders. The media crowded around Kabir, clicking his pictures, asking him to pose, hoping for a quick interview etc. An exhausted Sameer asked the coach for a doctor. He was now feeling ill. Needless to say, he couldn't attend the award ceremony.

Kabir was named 'Man of the Match' and was gifted a BMW and loads of cash. Sameer was forgotten.

The next day, the hospital nurse brought Sameer a newspaper. The headline screamed, 'Man of the Match – Kabir, gifts BMW to teammate Sameer!'

Think Tank

1. Why did Kabir gift his BMW to Sameer?

2. What can we learn from this story?

The Think Tank encourages you to answer these questions on your own before referring to the answers given below.

Answers

1. Whether anybody realized it or not, Kabir knew that had it not been for Sameer, they wouldn't have been able to win the match. Though Kabir had scored most of the runs and the last six in their partnership, Sameer had played the role of a stable, sound partner, encouraging Kabir whenever required. Here, Sameer had easily accepted a secondary role as a batsman and performed it in spite of his injury. Kabir respected and valued his contribution toward winning the match and that is why he wanted to share the prize with Sameer.

2. There are two lessons to be learnt here:

   i. Make the best of the situation like Sameer did. He was an amazing bowler but when the team required him as a batsman, he gave his best without thinking how difficult, tiring or painful it was.

   ii. When you achieve something great, also recognize the contribution of others in it. Their role and achievements may be smaller than yours but they may be the very foundation that you are standing on.

13

Manav,
the Meritorious Worker

Manav was a hardworking young boy who was employed in a printing company. He got along well with his team and his manager. Once, they were to deliver diaries at the beginning of the New Year. Since the job was urgent, his entire team was working overtime.

After the production was done, the team wrapped each diary and the order was ready for delivery the next afternoon. Late at around 11pm, Manav's team finished all the work and went home. Manav was to lock up the office. While leaving, he suddenly saw a bunch of labels which were left on the table. He realized that they had all forgotten to stick the labels on the wrapped diaries.

He realized that he would have to do it at that time itself. There was no way that they could complete the job if they started the next morning.

So he sat down and began to do the job by himself. It was around 11.30 pm when he was interrupted by a man in a safari suit. The man asked him what he was doing and Manav told him. He then asked the man who he was. The man said that he worked on the upper floors of the same company.

The man saw what he was doing and sat down to help him. They finished the job by 1 am, after which they went home.

The next day after they delivered the order, a peon came with an envelope for Manav from the Managing Director (MD), of the company. It had a cheque for ₹5,000/-.

Think Tank

1. Why had the MD of the company sent a cheque of ₹5,000 to Manav?

The Think Tank encourages you to answer the question on your own before referring to the answer given below.

Answer

1. The man in the safari suit was none other than the MD of the company. He had seen Manav complete his team's work instead of waiting for the others to arrive in the morning or calling his colleagues back to do the job. The MD wanted to reward him for his initiative and that is why he sent him a cheque.

14

The Little Pricks of Life

Life was tough in the jungle. Where survival of the fittest is the norm, no animal was fit any more. The cold that year was menacing. Most of the animals in the jungle had not survived.

The leader of the porcupines was worried. It was his duty to make sure that his people survived. He came up with a plan. He got together all the porcupines and told them that in order to stay warm, all of them had to stick together.

The porcupines were freezing. They agreed to do as he said. They all got together and stuck to each other. After sometime, they found that they could stay warm this way. Then, they became comfortable.

But after sometime, they began to feel uncomfortable. The problem was that their quills were all poking into each other. Thus, it was impossible for them to stay huddled together any longer. They went and complained about it to their leader.

To this, the leader said...

Think Tank

1. What was the leader's reply?

2. What is the moral of this story?

The Think Tank encourages you to answer these questions on your own before referring to the answers given below.

Answers

1. The leader said, 'You can either put up with the pricks of your own people and stay alive or die all alone of the cold. The choice is yours.'

2. The people who are closest to us have the power to hurt us the most. But they are also the ones who can help us get out of life-threatening situations. Whether to put up with their prickly quills and live happily, or to be alone and face everything all by ourselves is our choice.

15

The Right Decision

Suspense was in the air. Whom would King Dhritarashtra appoint as the crown prince – his own son Duryodhan, or Yudhisthir, the son of his late brother, King Pandu? In spite of being the firstborn, his younger brother Pandu had been crowned king, as Dhritarashtra had been born blind. But later, when Pandu renounced the throne, Dhritarashtra sat on the throne as his representative. Even after Pandu's untimely death, Dhritarashtra continued to act on his behalf.

Some felt that since Duryodhan was the eldest son of the ruling king, Dhritarashtra, he should be appointed the crown prince. However, Yudhisthir was the eldest son of the earlier King Pandu and he was also elder to Duryodhan. Additionally, he was also righteous by nature. Dharma was his middle name. Many felt that he should be appointed crown prince because he would be a righteous king.

The day of the announcement arrived. Everybody had gathered in the royal court to hear the king's decision. At that time, four prisoners were brought into the court by the guards. One of the guards explained that all four of them had been arrested on the charge of murdering a man. Vidur, the king's advisor, announced that both Duryodhan and Yudhisthir be given a chance to pronounce their verdict on the punishment to be awarded to the four accused. This way, they would be able to prove their capability for the position of crown prince.

Duryodhan, being arrogant, stated that he should have the first chance, as he was the son of King Dhritarashtra. He announced his decision that the law of the kingdom – that a murderer would be given the death sentence, would apply in this case.

This gladdened the hearts of his supporters. Vidur then asked the king to give Yudhisthir a chance. King Dhritarashtra, clearly in favour of his own son, asked Vidur how Yudhisthir could have anything different to say. However, Vidur persisted and Yudhisthir was given a chance.

To everyone's surprise, Yudhisthir asked to know the castes of the accused. The four murderers belonged to the four different castes – one was a Brahmin (from the community of learned men); one, a Kshatriya (from the community of warriors); one, a Vaishya (from the merchant community), and one, a Shudra (from the lower-most caste of people).

Yudhisthir declared four years of imprisonment for the Shudra, eight years for the Vaishya and sixteen years for the Kshatriya. As per the law of the kingdom, a Brahmin could not be given a death sentence and so he asked their *Kulguru* to decide the Brahmin's punishment. His verdict puzzled everyone. He was asked to explain the reason behind his verdict.

Yudhisthir gave his reasons and was appointed crown prince.

Think Tank

1. What was the reason behind Yudhisthir's judgement?

2. Why was Duryodhan unable to come up with the righteous verdict?

The Think Tank encourages you to answer these questions on your own before referring to the answers given below.

Answers

1. The Shudras were not expected to be knowledgeable about Dharma and laws. So, the Shudra was awarded only four years of imprisonment. A Vaishya was supposed to be more knowledgeable than a Shudra. Therefore, his crime was higher than that committed by the Shudra. So, he was given double the punishment given to the Shudra i.e., eight years of imprisonment. A Kshatriya was supposed to protect people. For him, committing a murder was a sin higher than that for a Vaishya. So, he was given double the punishment given to a Vaishya i.e.,16 years of imprisonment. A Brahmin was the most learned among all the four castes. Committing murder was a higher sin for him as compared to the rest. So he deserved the highest punishment which would be decided by the *Kulguru*.

2. Duryodhan wanted to be the king by hook or crook. Neither was he knowledgeable about Dharma, nor was he interested in being an able and righteous leader to his people. Thus, he was unable to think beyond the usual laws.

16

We Believe in You

Sagar was one of the most valued employees in his company. A hard worker, he was well-known for his ability to complete tough projects. He had the courage to make tough decisions, good people skills to accomplish tasks, and the patience to see projects through.

Once, his firm had submitted a tender for a prestigious but extremely challenging project. Sagar had worked on the tender and the finer points required for its completion. He was quite confident of executing and completing the project to perfection.

His company was awarded the project. A celebration was organized and the CEO was to give a speech on the occasion. The CEO was a people's person and was popular across the organization.

Sagar too, was very pleased with this development and was looking forward to begin work on the project. Before the celebration, Sagar's boss called him for a briefing on the project. He said, 'I hope you haven't bitten off more than you can chew, young man. This is the most challenging project you have ever come across. And the CEO too is watching you. I just hope you don't fall flat on your face.'

On hearing this, Sagar suddenly began to doubt himself. A chill crept up his spine. Had he been overconfident? Was he really capable of executing the project? But how could he back out now? The company had bagged the project and it was a known fact that he was going to execute it. What could he possibly do now?

He thought of telling the management that he wouldn't do the job after all and that the project should be handed over to someone else. While he was thinking about it, his colleagues came to call him for the celebration.

In a while, the CEO arrived. He began by congratulating Sagar's team on bagging such a prestigious project. He went on to say how challenging it was and that it was a never-before project undertaken by the company. Sagar's confidence was at an all-time low. He felt like telling the CEO that he was not going to do the project after all.

And then, the CEO said a few words which made him smile. His confidence was restored and once more he began to look forward to starting work on the project.

Think Tank

1. What did the CEO say that restored Sagar's confidence?

2. What is the moral of this story?

The Think Tank encourages you to answer these questions on your own before referring to the answers given below.

Answers

1. The CEO's words were, 'We believe in you, Sagar. We are all with you.'

2. The CEO was a great leader. He knew that even a great performer needs words of encouragement from his seniors. Though the project's success majorly depended on Sagar, the CEO's belief in him was instrumental in restoring his confidence, as opposed to his boss' attitude which caused him to question his capabilities.

17

Chanakya – The Perfect State Official

Chanakya is known as a great philosopher, strategist and teacher in ancient Indian history. The author of the work *Arthashastra*, he also served as advisor to Chandragupta whom he had helped to become king.

One day, while he was working late, a traveller came to meet him. Chanakya was busy and asked his guest to wait till he was free. As his guest waited before him, Chanakya completed his work in the light of an oil lamp.

When he had finished, he put out the oil lamp he was using. He then lighted another and then began his meeting with the guest. The guest was quite surprised and asked him why he had put out the lamp he was working with and then lit another.

─────────── **Think Tank** ───────────

1. What was Chanakya's reply?

2. What is the implication of this story?

The Think Tank encourages you to answer these questions on your own before referring to the answers given below.

Answers

1. Chanakya told him that the oil lamp was a necessary resource given to him by the kingdom to fulfil his duties as an official. However, meeting the guest was work of a personal nature and it was wrong on his part to use official resources for personal work.

2. In an age where misappropriation of national resources for personal gains is the order of the day, Chanakya had set an excellent example with his clear thinking and conscientious behaviour.

18

Who is Ram Kumar?

Raman and Rajendra were batchmates at an MBA college. They had both been selected by a company as management trainees. After working for a year, they were to be appraised and promoted based on their performances.

Both of them performed well consistently throughout the year. Then came the time for their appraisal. Only one of them could be promoted to the position of Assistant Manager-Sales. At this position, they had to handle a small team and report to the Manager-Sales.

Since both of them were competent in all other respects, the Manager-Sales wanted to choose the person with leadership qualities, as the Assistant Manager-Sales was supposed to handle a team. This would be a new step in their careers.

He designed a test for them. The one who passed the test would be promoted to the position of Assistant Manager-Sales. He called both of them to his cabin and said, 'There is a person called Ram Kumar in our organization. I want both of you to find out who he is and what he does. You have one day's time to find him.'

Both Raman and Rajendra were excited. Rajendra made a beeline to the HR department to get the list of employees in each department, while Raman did nothing.

Both of them were ready with their answers the next day. Rajendra confidently told the Manager-Sales that there was no such person called Ram Kumar who worked for the organization. He told the manager that he had been through the list of employees in various departments but had found no such person. The manager then asked Raman for his answer.

Raman said he had found Ram Kumar and brought him in to meet the manager. A shocked Rajendra looked into the face of Ram Kumar – the aged peon who served them tea daily.

Think Tank

1. How had Raman found Ram Kumar, while Rajendra hadn't?

2. What is the moral of the story?

The Think Tank encourages you to answer these questions on your own before referring to the answers given below.

Answers

1. Rajendra had conveniently assumed that Ram Kumar was working in some department in the organization. It didn't strike him to look around him or that his boss meant a peon in the office. Thus, he did not find him. On the other hand, Raman already knew Ram Kumar from his daily interactions

with him. He did not presume that his boss meant someone more important and at a higher level than a peon.

2. For a leader, it is important to know his people. Be it a top-ranking executive or a peon, every person in the organization adds value to it. It is important for a leader to know and to take care of each and every person around him, irrespective of his position in the organization. Raman proved to have the qualities of a good leader and so was promoted.

19

Right Man for the Right Job

Sukarna was an orphan. He was raised by the village priest. He grew up to be an honest and hardworking boy. After completing his education, the priest asked him to start something of his own for his livelihood.

Sukarna decided to sell flowers to the people coming to the temple. The priest sent him to one of his relatives who sold flowers, to learn the business. The man showed Sukarna how to select flowers, make garlands and arrange flowers beautifully. He also showed him the tricks of the trade – how to arrange slightly wilted flowers along with fresh ones, how to leave gaps in the garlands to save on the flowers used etc.

Sukarna came back to his village and started his business. But from the very beginning, he incurred losses. Though the people were happy with the quality of flowers and garlands he sold, he did not earn a profit for himself. He was unable to negotiate with people from whom he purchased flowers. He also did not find it ethical to use tricks of the trade and use wilted flowers and leave gaps in the garlands. He soon had to close down his shop.

Next, he started selling snacks. But once again, he wasn't able to run his business. People came to buy snacks from him because they knew him to be honest and that he would sell items of good quality, but again, he couldn't maintain his quality and yet make a profit for himself.

Soon he came to be known as honest, hardworking and good-for-nothing! The priest was disappointed in him. Sukarna too felt that he was absolutely useless. The priest's friend Swamy, who owned the only grocery store in the village was watching Sukarna's struggle with great interest.

One day, Swamy came to meet Sukarna at his home. He told him that he was going to start a second grocery store in the village. He needed someone to handle the new store. He offered Sukarna the job. Both, the priest and Sukarna were surprised.

The priest told Swamy that having closed down two businesses already, Sukarna was an unlikely candidate to handle a store profitably. Swamy only said, 'Sukarna, you just take up the job. Leave the profitability to me.'

His judgement turned out to be correct and the store was a huge success.

Think Tank

1. How did Swamy know that Sukarna would succeed at handling the new store?

The Think Tank encourages you to answer the question on your own before referring to the answer given below.

Answer

1. A businessman or a leader must be able to identify the right man for the right job. Swamy realized that the problem with Sukarna was only that he did not have a business mindset. He had the mindset of a good employee. He would do as he was told with honesty and sincerity. Additionally, people believed that Sukarna would give them best quality goods. Since he was honest, Swamy could trust him completely with the stock and the money. Swamy looked after the profitability of the store while Sukarna handled the day-to-day tasks. Thus, Swamy chose the right man for the right job and was rewarded.

20

The Family Called India

A huge mob stopped the bus. But nobody had the guts to leave the bus and asked them why. The driver and the conductor were both worried about the safety of the bus and the passengers.

Communal riots were the order of the day. Raheem, the conductor had been worried yesterday as soon as he had heard the news. He had even talked to the management of the state transport where he worked, to cancel all trips on this route. But the management depended on orders from their higher-ups and could take no decisions on their own.

Raheem looked at the frames of the various gods which the driver, Shambhu had lined up near the steering wheel. He prayed to gods of both faiths to save them all.

Armed with weapons of various kinds, the mob had stopped the bus, but they hadn't done it any harm yet. 'Why?' wondered Raheem. Apparently, they were waiting for their leader. As soon as the leader came, the mob stood ready to do his bidding. A man with a deep-set face, he looked as though he was born with a scowl.

The passengers meanwhile were saying their prayers. 'Will they kill us all?' an old man wondered aloud. 'Not if we can help it,' declared Raheem. 'Listen, and do as I say,' he said.

The leader banged hard on the door of the bus. 'Open up!' he bellowed. Raheem steeled himself and opened the door. The leader came in holding a sword menacingly at Raheem's throat. 'Hindus and Muslims, stand separately,' he said. Nobody moved. 'Are you guys deaf?' he hollered. 'Hindus and Muslims stand separately!' Yet nobody moved. 'Do you want us to kill all of you?' he went on.

'Yes!' they all answered in unison.

Raheem spoke on their behalf. The leader froze in his tracks. A few minutes later, the bus was on its way again.

Think Tank

1. What did Raheem say to the leader?

2. Why did the leader let them go?

The Think Tank encourages you to answer these questions on your own before referring to the answers given below.

Answers

1. Raheem said it was impossible for them to divide themselves into Hindus and Muslims as they were all members of a big, huge family called India. This family had no single religion. Raheem told him, 'If you are a Hindu, treat us as Muslims and kill us. If you are a Muslim, treat us as Hindus and kill us. But you will have to kill us all.'

2. Raheem's statement was an eye-opener for the leader. He saw

that the members of this family called India were ready to die for each other. He realized that he and his fellowmen too were a part of this huge family called India. The secular spirit of all the people in the bus had broken down his resolution to kill those who belonged to a faith other than his, and he let them go.

COURAGE

21

No Time for Fear

Nikhil always teased Rohan about being a 'scaredy-cat'. Rohan never protested. He knew he was one. He was afraid of the dark, thunder, lightning, dogs and even of talking to strangers. Nikhil, about five years elder to Rohan, was bold, dashing and courageous. Rohan adored his elder brother and wished he could someday be as courageous as him.

Late one evening, while they were cycling home on a deserted road, a two-wheeler coming from the opposite direction rammed into their cycle. The man on the two-wheeler was terrified and got away. Rohan was badly hurt, but Nikhil had fainted! Rohan tried to revive Nikhil but he couldn't. Rohan realized there was no time to lose. It was already dark and home was quite far away.

He moved Nikhil to the side of the road and taking the cycle, went to find help at a furious pace. Suddenly, it started raining and he could see lightning. I must go faster, he thought. He pedalled faster till he came to a few houses. He asked where he could find a doctor. Fortunately, the doctor lived nearby in a bungalow down the road. There was a huge dog standing at the entrance. Rohan decided he had to go in irrespective of the dog. Shivering due to the rain, he went ahead bravely. He expected the dog to leap on him, but thankfully it was chained to the kennel. The doctor went in his car with Rohan and took Nikhil to a hospital.

When Nikhil was better, his parents told him the whole story. He was surprised that his kid brother, 'scaredy-cat' had courageously faced the fact that he had fainted, cycled through the rain in the dark to find a doctor and bravely gone into the bungalow in spite of the huge dog.

'How did you do it? Weren't you scared?' asked Nikhil.

Think Tank

1. What was Rohan's reply?

2. How had Rohan suddenly become courageous that day?

The Think Tank encourages you to answer these questions on your own before referring to the answers given below.

Answers

1. Rohan told Nikhil that all he could see was that his beloved brother needed help immediately and that it was up to him to save Nikhil come what may. The dark, the rain, lightning, strangers, the dog, nothing was more important than his brother's life. There was no time for fear.

2. In view of the most important thing, saving his brother's life, Rohan had blocked out all other doubts and fears from his mind. It wasn't as if he could have overpowered the dog, but he was ready to face the danger with courage if it meant getting to the doctor and helping save Nikhil.

22

Helping an Old Lady

Rajesh suffered from panic attacks. He would be scared to go out alone on his own or travel long distances. Sometimes, the attacks were so severe that he couldn't even do something as simple as going out to the grocer nearby. Though he was 19, he wasn't like other kids of his age who went along with their friends and had fun.

He was on medication and was determined to overcome this problem, but at times it worked and at times it didn't. When it didn't, he would be very upset and his confidence would be shattered. His friends, relatives and doctor tried to help him get over it, but nobody could find a lasting solution to this problem.

One day, his mother asked him to go and book railway tickets for her. After much persuasion, he went. While on his way, he found that a huge crowd had gathered around an old lady. She had been knocked down by a car and was bleeding profusely. He saw her and realized it was the old granny who lived alone next door. Her only son lived in another town. Nobody in the crowd knew her.

Rajesh acted fast. He took her to a nearby hospital where the doctors told him she needed blood. He made all the necessary arrangements, called up her son, arranged for the money and bought her medicines. Then he waited till his parents came to the hospital.

After the old granny was out of danger, Rajesh's mother asked him how he had been able to do all these things for the old granny on his own, when he was scared to even go and book a ticket by himself.

Think Tank
---

1. What was Rajesh's answer?

The Think Tank encourages you to answer the question on your own before referring to the answer given below.

Answer

1. Rajesh answered that all he could see was that granny's life depended on being admitted to the hospital immediately, and there was nobody else besides him to do it. Thus, it was no longer a question of whether he could do it or not; he just had to. Once his mind realized this, there was absolutely no place for any fear.

23

Royal Treatment

During his conquests in India, Alexander the Great fought a great battle with King Porus. Porus was a brave Indian king who had dared to oppose Alexander despite knowing that the odds were against him. No other king was ready to support him at the time.

In spite of this, Porus stood up to Alexander and put up a tough fight. He lost most of his troops in battle and also his sons. Finally, he was captured and brought to Alexander.

Alexander had heard quite a bit about Porus and knew him to be a brave and courageous king. In spite of his defeat, Porus stood regally before Alexander, his confidence and pride intact.

Alexander then asked him, 'How do you wish I should treat you, O Porus?'

Think Tank
---

1. What was the reply Porus gave him?

2. What effect did it have on Alexander?

The Think Tank encourages you to answer these questions on your own before referring to the answers given below.

Answers

1. The brave King Porus replied, 'Treat me, like a king ought to be treated.'

2. Alexander was impressed with these words of Porus and his courage. As per his wish, Alexander treated Porus like a king. In spite of his defeat, Porus retained his status as king though he owed allegiance to Alexander.

24

Hirkani

This is the story of a courageous milkmaid called Hirkani who lived during the reign of Shivaji Maharaj. Every day she climbed up the path to the tall fort built by Shivaji Maharaj to sell milk and came back home to her little son in the evening.

Shivaji Maharaj had issued strict orders that the doors of the fort were to be closed in the evening for security reasons and that nobody should be allowed to come in or go out after that. These orders were strictly followed by the soldiers.

One evening, after selling milk, Hirkani came to the door of the fort quite late, after it had been closed for the day. As per the rules, the guards refused to allow her to pass. She pleaded with them to allow her to go, as her young son was at home and he could not stay alone. But they refused. They told her that the door would remain closed for the night and she would be able to leave only the next day.

Hirkani knew that there was no way her son could stay alone without her. She just had to reach home. She then remembered another path which was near a watch tower. However, the watch tower was deserted because it was simply impossible for anyone, even the most experienced soldiers to use that path. She decided to go down that way.

The odds were stacked against her. It was already dark. The path was known to be too dangerous to use and she was a mere milkmaid. It was an impossible feat!

But Hirkani gathered her courage. She knew she had to go down that path and reach her son. She made up her mind, courageously faced all the dangers in her path and finally reached home.

Think Tank

1. How did Hirkani go down the path that was impossible for even trained soldiers?

2. How did Shivaji Maharaj react on hearing her feat?

The Think Tank encourages you to answer these questions on your own before referring to the answers given below.

Answers

1. We are capable of showing tremendous courage when our loved ones are threatened. The same happened in Hirkani's case. She realized that the guards would not allow her to go and her son would be alone. In order to reach him, she blocked out everything else, the difficulty of the path, lack of training to climb down, the darkness and all other dangers.

2. Shivaji Maharaj reprimanded the guards for not letting a mother leave to reach her son. He also rewarded Hirkani for her bravery. The watch tower from where she descended was named Hirkani *Buruj* in her honour and to date is known by her name. The word 'Hirkani' is also used in the Marathi language to denote a mother who can achieve amazing feats for her children.

25

Why Can't We…?

Ramani's husband had been an Army man. He had died on duty. Her son had just entered his teens that year.

Over the years, Ramani got over her grief and so did her son. When the time came for him to choose a career, he told her that he too would like to join the Army and dedicate his life to serving his country, like his father had done.

Ramani threw a fit. 'What! Did I struggle so much all these years without your father, just to hear you say that you too want to join the Army? I can't live with you being away for months together.'

Her in-laws tried to persuade her to let her son take up the career of his choice, but to no avail. 'I had to live without my husband all these years! Am I to live in anxiety for my son's life too?' she asked.

'We too have lost our son, my dear,' pointed out her mother-in-law.

'All the more reason for me to ensure that I don't lose mine! Sorry son, but after losing your father, I cannot take this anxiety of living for months without you. And further, I have no courage left to lose you too.'

Her son's answer stunned her.

Think Tank

1. What was her son's answer?

The Think Tank encourages you to answer the question on your own before referring to the answer given below.

Answer

1. He said, 'Mother, if even people with evil designs have the courage to give up their lives for their evil causes, why can't we have the courage to dedicate our lives for the right cause?'

26

The Brave Soldier

This is the story of a soldier of the Gurkha Infantry, Bishnu Shrestha. After his retirement, he was travelling to his home in Nepal by train. In the dead of the night, around 40 armed ruffians entered the train with the intention of looting it. They looted passengers and also tried to molest a young, 18-year-old girl.

That's when Bishnu interrupted them. Using his *kukri* knife, he valiantly fought the intruders, killing three of them and wounding many others. The rest of the ruffians saw this and ran for their lives. Bishnu suffered a serious injury to his left hand. The grateful parents of the young girl wanted to give Bishnu a huge cash reward.

But he denied it saying…

―――――――――― **Think Tank** ――――――――――

1. What did Bishnu say?

―――――――――――――――――――――――――――――――――――

The Think Tank encourages you to answer the question on your own before referring to the answer given below.

Answer

1. Bishnu said, 'Fighting the enemy is my duty as a soldier. Taking on the thugs was my duty as a human being!'

WISDOM

27

The Power of Knowledge

Once upon a time, there was a girl called Swaroopa. She was a very learned and intelligent girl from a middle-class family. After her studies were done, her parents began to look out for a suitable groom for her.

However, many of the alliances that came her way were of boys who were not as intelligent or learned as she was. This was the reason that many of them rejected her proposal. This made her parents very sad. Her grandfather consulted an astrologer who told him that her birth chart was auspicious and that she would soon get married into a suitable family and would travel to many lands with her husband.

Soon after, they received two matrimonial alliances. One was from the house of a royal courtier. His son was said to be brave and he too held a place of influence in the king's court. The other boy was very learned and came from a family of teachers. Though not in the service of the king, they were well-known for their knowledge and widely respected for their advice and counsel.

Both the families arranged to see Swaroopa and they were both eager to finalize the marriage. Swaroopa too, thought that both the boys were equal in all respects. Now her father was worried. He asked his father, i.e. Swaroopa's grandfather for his opinion. Who was the right match for Swaroopa? The grandfather told him to finalize Swaroopa's marriage to the learned boy.

Think Tank

1. Why did the grandfather choose the learned boy over the brave courtier who was in service with the king?

The Think Tank encourages you to answer the question on your own before referring to the answer given below.

Answer

1. Her grandfather knew that Swaroopa would travel to various lands with her husband. He chose the learned boy over the other boy who was in service at the king's court because he knew that a learned man gains respect and influence wherever he goes, whereas, a person in service with the king will wield influence and gain respect only in the kingdom where he serves.

28

The Reality of Life

Shruti's son Siddharth lived and worked in the city, while the rest of their family lived in the village. Recently, she had heard all sorts of things about him from well-wishers. He was supposed to be having a good time – late-night parties, weird friends and all the things a mother doesn't want to hear about her son.

She confided to her brother Ram, that she was worried about her son. Ram was a wise man. He decided to go to the city and see if what she had heard was true. When he arrived, he found Siddharth surprised to see him. However, he welcomed him. Ram told Siddharth that he would stay that day. He took one look at Siddharth's house and knew that his sister's fears had come true.

They had food, chatted and went to sleep. The next day, as Ram got ready to leave, he asked Siddharth, 'Will you help me tie my shoelaces?' Siddharth was quite surprised but he helped his uncle with the shoelaces. Ram heaved a huge sigh and said…

―――――――――― **Think Tank** ――――――――――

1. What did Ram say?

2. What was the effect of his words on Siddharth?

The Think Tank encourages you to answer these questions on your own before referring to the answers given below.

Answers

1. Ram said, 'Thank you, child. One only gets weaker day-by-day. Take care.'

2. His words hit Siddharth like a ton of bricks. He realized that the reality of life was that it was passing by and each day, he too was moving towards old age. He understood that instead of valuing his life, he was wiling it away with his actions.

29

Calming Down a Disturbed Mind

Once, Buddha and his disciples stopped for rest near a lake. Buddha asked one of his disciples to fetch him some water as he was thirsty. The disciple went to the lake. However, he saw that just then there were some people washing clothes in the lake, others were washing animals, and yet another man was taking a bullock cart across the lake. The water had become very muddy due to this. The disciple returned to Buddha saying that it was impossible to drink the water from the lake.

After about half an hour, Buddha sent the disciple once again to the lake. He came back again saying that the water was too muddy to be drunk.

After some time, Buddha sent the same disciple again to bring him water from the same lake. This time, the water was clear and looked clean. The disciple then brought some water for Buddha.

Buddha asked his disciple, 'What did you do to make the water clear?'

The disciple said, 'I did nothing. I just let it be and it cleared on its own.'

Think Tank

1. What can we learn from this story?

_____

The Think Tank encourages you to answer the question on your own before referring to the answer given below.

Answer

1. Just like the mud in the water settled down on its own when it was left alone, the mind too when disturbed, will settle down on its own when you leave it alone. Giving it time is the best solution.

30

The Power of Small

A group of safety pins were talking to one another. The biggest among them had captivated the audience. 'And as I sat on the lady's shoulder, attached to her sari, I saw the wonderful party. There was lots of food, drinks, music and merriment...' it went on. A slim and decorated safety pin haughtily ventured, 'I too have had wonderful experiences. I am not just a safety pin, I am actually a brooch. I am used only on the best of occasions and only for the best of silk saris. See, I am wrapped up in plastic too, unlike the rest of you.'

Each safety pin went on to relate its experience. A young, tiny safety pin was intrigued and also disappointed by this. It had no experience. It had been given to the lady of the house by her mother and had been separated from its brothers and sisters. Now it was bored, lying in a box without them. Moreover, the others had had fantastic experiences, while it had had none. 'Don't you have any experience to relate?' said the haughty safety pin to the little safety pin. 'I have never been outside,' the little pin replied.

'Of course, of what use would a tiny little fellow like you be? You don't stand much chance of gaining experience either,' said the haughty safety pin.

This pushed the small safety pin into the depths of sorrow. A wise old safety pin observed the disappointment on its face and said, 'Never fear. Your time shall come too. Each one of us has its own use.' But the young safety pin was still disappointed. It couldn't believe it was of use to anybody.

One day, there was a party in the house. All the safety pins were very happy as it was an opportunity to get out of their box. However, the dress code was western formals and the safety pins were not required that day. All of them sat thoroughly disappointed. Just then, the lady of the house came looking for her safety pin box. 'Quick, we need a safety pin for the Mayor's spectacles,' she told her friend. 'A little screw has fallen off them and he can't wear them now. Such an important man too. I must find a safety pin for him right away!'

As she opened the box, all the safety pins stood tall and proud vying for her attention. It was such an honour for a safety pin to be of use to the Mayor. The little safety pin however, didn't even get up. It felt it stood no chance. The lady moved all the other bigger safety pins aside…

---------------   **Think Tank**   ---------------

1. Can you guess what happened next?

2. What is the implication of this story?

The Think Tank encourages you to answer these questions on your own before referring to the answers given below.

Answers

1. The Mayor's spectacles needed a tiny safety pin to be held together. Thus, much to the disappointment of the big and shiny safety pins, the lady chose the tiny little safety pin for this important mission. The wise old safety pin's words had come true.

2. All of us whether big or small are important in our own way and have our own roles to play. Nobody is inferior or superior to others. All of us are here to fulfil our own purpose.

31

A Matter of Tact

Soni and her friend were extremely tired. They had just completed their journey of over five hours by bus. Extremely hungry and feeling terribly hot, they decided that dinner was the next thing on their agenda. Near the station, they found an expensive-looking restaurant. Soni remembered that the restaurant was well-known for serving the best fish in town. However, since it served vegetarian food as well, they decided to go there.

They were able to get a place after fifteen minutes of waiting. Since it was Sunday evening, it was packed to the gills and the owner himself was helping out, taking orders. He came to their table with a smile and asked them for their order. They had already decided that they wouldn't go for the regular *roti sabji*. Instead, they ordered two *alu parathas*. The owner looked agitated. He thought that on a busy Sunday evening, where people had lined up to have fish meals, all these girls wanted were *alu parathas*! He said he would have to check if they could be provided.

After some moments he came back and grudgingly told them that they *could* manage two *alu parathas*, though they were up to their necks in preparing that day's special which was fish curry.

As they came close to finishing the *alu parathas*, Soni and her friend realized that they needed two more *parathas* to satisfy their hunger. However, judging by the owner's earlier reaction, Soni doubted he would be ready to prepare two more *alu parathas*. However, both of them were hungry and not at all eager to have non-veg food.

Soon, the owner came and asked if they would like to order anything else. Soni asked for what she wanted. The owner suddenly smiled, assured her that it was no problem at all and went to get them two *alu parathas*.

_____ **Think Tank** _____

1. What did Soni say that made the owner smile and rush to get them two *alu parathas*?

2. What is the implication of this story?

The Think Tank encourages you to answer these questions on your own before referring to the answers given below.

Answers

1. Soni said, 'The *alu parathas* were delicious. I have never tasted such good *alu parathas* before. We would love to have two more, but it's not fair on my part to ask you for them, right?'

2. If you want a person to do something for you, you must tell him in a way that he wants to hear. The owner was thrilled to hear that his restaurant served the best *alu parathas*. He began to feel it was an honour to serve them to someone who appreciated them so much. There was simply no question of refusing the order.

32

The Sneakers

Aditi was in the twelfth standard. She was good at studies and equally fond of cooking. Her mother ran a catering business. That month was the peak season for the business and her mother was short of help.

One day, Aditi came home and told her father that she wanted ₹2000 to buy a pair of sneakers. Now Aditi had four pairs of shoes and her parents wondered what she wanted sneakers for. She wasn't interested in going to a gym or running. But all Aditi's friends wore sneakers and she too had to have them. She said she felt too out of place among her friends without the sneakers.

Instead of refusing outright, her father made her an offer. Aditi had Christmas holidays for ten days and her mother needed help in her work. He asked Aditi to help her mother in her business for ten days. Her mother would pay her for her help. Her father told her that she could buy the sneakers with the money that she earned by working with her mother. The shortfall would be paid by him.

Aditi thought it was a good idea. She began to help her mother. She had to get up daily at 5 am, and help her mother with everything, right from peeling vegetables, grinding masalas, washing vessels and anything else that was required. Starting their work at

6 am, they finished each day by 6 pm. Aditi was completely exhausted at the end of each day.

Her mother was very happy with her work. She decided to pay Aditi, ₹1000 for her work of ten days. Her father too was pleased that Aditi had helped her mother. He told Aditi that next Sunday they would go to buy her the sneakers she wanted. He would pay the difference of ₹1000 for the sneakers.

Aditi looked at him with a strange expression and said...

Think Tank

1. What did Aditi say to her father?

2. What is the implication of this story?

The Think Tank encourages you to answer these questions on your own before referring to the answers given below.

Answers

1. Aditi said, 'What! Do you want me to spend my hard-earned money on a pair of sneakers?'

2. Until we earn money by doing hard work ourselves, we do not realize its true value. Till Aditi's father was paying for the sneakers, she didn't realize the value of money. But when she saw how hard she had to work to earn a thousand rupees, she realized its true value and decided that the sneakers were not worth spending her hard-earned money on.

33

In My Opinion...

Dr. Vishwas was an expert in clinical psychology. He had also brought many new ideas to light. These ideas had been proven through his experiments. However, the older and accomplished people in his profession were a little alarmed by these new ideas of his and were still not ready to accept them.

One of them was Dr. Vishwas' teacher, Dr. Mehta. He completely opposed Dr. Vishwas' findings and his 'newfangled ideas', as he called them. He wondered what the world was coming to by ignoring the earlier theories of clinical psychology.

At a conference, Dr. Vishwas was felicitated for his great discoveries. At this time, one of his fellow associates asked him what his opinion about Dr. Mehta was.

Dr. Vishwas said, 'I think Dr. Mehta is a very accomplished researcher and a very good teacher as well. His research has been the foundation of many treatments to date.'

The associate was surprised and asked him, 'How can you say so? Dr. Mehta has a very bad opinion about you and moreover, he also brings it up at almost every occasion.'

The associate was stunned with Dr. Vishwas' reply.

Think Tank
---

1. What did Dr. Vishwas say?

The Think Tank encourages you to answer the question on your own before referring to the answer given below.

Answer

1. Dr. Vishwas said, 'Well, you asked me for *my* opinion of Dr. Mehta. It has nothing to do with *his* opinion about me.'

34

A Handful of Praise

Sameera's cousins from the US were coming to stay with her for a week. Though she was happy about it, she was also very worried. Had she been at her parent's home it would have been no problem at all. But at her in-laws' place...

Her father-in-law was not a problem and neither was her husband or brother-in-law. But *Sasuji*...! She was a strict disciplinarian and wasn't very fond of people visiting them. She thought people disturbed the system of her home. And though she said nothing to Sameera, Sameera was sure she would definitely find fault with her cousins!

When her cousins had called to tell her that they would be visiting her, she hadn't been able to refuse. Neither could she ask her cousins to cancel their visit, nor was she sure her mother-in-law would welcome them.

She asked her friend how to tackle this problem. Her friend told her the way out. When her cousins came, she first took them to her mother-in-law's room and introduced her mother-in-law to them.

Sameera's mother-in-law behaved like the perfect host and was very loving towards them. Her cousins' visit was a great success.

Think Tank

1. What did Sameera do to change her mother-in-law's attitude towards her cousins?

2. What is the moral of this story?

The Think Tank encourages you to answer these questions on your own before referring to the answers given below.

Answers

1. While introducing her mother-in-law to her cousins, Sameera described her as a very caring and loving person. She also told them how her mother-in-law was more of a mother to her rather than a mother-in-law.

2. People have a habit of living up to your expectations. If you tell them that you expect the best out of them, they are motivated to do their best. This is what Sameera did. Through her words, she conveyed her high expectations of her mother-in-law's behaviour to her, as well as her cousins. Her mother-in-law behaved accordingly.

MATURITY

35

You See What You Are

Raj and Viraj were studying under a guru and lived in his ashram. Raj was a good boy, truthful, trustworthy and good-tempered, while Viraj was wicked, told lies and was bad-tempered.

One day, the guru gave them a task. He asked both of them to go out of the ashram. Raj was to look for a bad person, find him and bring him to the ashram. Viraj was told to find a good person and bring him back with him to the ashram.

Both of them left for this task. After three months of searching, they came back. The guru asked Raj, 'Did you find a bad person, my boy?'

'No, Guruji,' answered Raj. 'I looked everywhere but couldn't find any bad person anywhere.'

Next, the guru asked Viraj, 'Did you find a good person, my boy?'

'No, Guruji,' answered Viraj. 'I looked everywhere but couldn't find any good person anywhere.'

Think Tank

1. What is the moral of this story?

The Think Tank encourages you to answer the question on your own before referring to the answer given below.

Answer

1. What we see around us is a reflection of our inner state. Raj saw the reflection of his inner state – goodness, in everyone he met and so couldn't find a single bad person. Viraj saw the reflection of his inner state – wickedness, in everyone he met and so couldn't find a single good person.

36

The Unprofessional Doctor

Raghavan was extremely worried. His son, Aditya had to be operated upon that day. It was a critical operation. His son meant the world to him and although, he tried to comfort Aditya who was petrified, he himself was quite agitated.

The nurse had readied Aditya but the doctor hadn't arrived yet. 'Why hasn't the doctor come yet?' complained Raghavan to the nurse.

'He'll be here in a short while,' she answered.

'Isn't he aware that my son must be operated upon immediately? My son is scared to death. How long must he wait for the dreaded operation to start?' shouted Raghavan.

'We'll begin as soon as the doctor is here,' said the nurse.

About fifteen minutes later, the doctor arrived rushing to get ready for the operation. 'About time you came in, Doctor. My son has been waiting for so long and he's scared out of his wits,' said Raghavan sarcastically. The doctor said nothing.

'I hope my son is going to be okay. You must do your best, Doctor.'

'I will do my best, Mr. Raghavan. The rest is in God's hands,' said the doctor.

'It's my child at stake, Doctor. Please don't pass on the responsibility to God. *You* must do your best,' said Raghavan. The doctor nodded patiently.

'It's so easy for him to be calm. It's not his child!' muttered Raghavan under his breath.

Once the operation was over, Raghavan was relieved. In retrospect, he thought he had been too harsh on the doctor. He looked around for him to thank him but again, he was nowhere to be found. He asked the nurse. She told him that he had already left. Raghavan was enraged. 'Why didn't he even stop to speak to me after the operation? How unprofessional of him!'

The nurse looked at him and said, 'He came because the operation was urgent. He has just lost his son. He was making arrangements for his last rites!'

Think Tank

1. What is the moral of this story?

The Think Tank encourages you to answer the question on your own before referring to the answer given below.

Answer

1. It is easy to blame someone because they don't act as per our expectations — like Raghavan blamed the doctor. But if we

think about it, we shall understand that everybody has their own difficulties which may be much more serious than ours. The doctor had put aside his personal grief and come to do his duty. But Raghavan, in his anxiety hadn't been able to think that the doctor too may have been late due to some problem.

37

The Right Woman

Richa had just completed her post-graduation and landed a good job in a multinational company in her city. She had a 'Work Hard, Party Harder' mindset like most others of her generation. After a year of working, her parents decided to look for a suitable boy for her.

Richa began to think about what kind of a husband she wanted. Her parents arranged for suitable boys and their families to meet them. However, they found that Richa rejected all of them. They were either too tall, too short, too fat, too thin, silly, idiotic etc. A year passed by this way.

Once Richa went to her grandmother's house to stay for a few days. The topic of her marriage came up. Her grandmother asked her what the developments on that front were.

Richa answered, 'Oh! Nothing as yet!'

Her granny asked her what was taking so long.

Richa answered, 'I am looking for the right man, granny.'

Her granny looked at her and said…

1. What did Richa's granny say to her?

2. What is the implication of this story?

The Think Tank encourages you to answer these questions on your own before referring to the answers given below.

Answers

1. Richa's granny said, 'Don't look for the right man; you won't find him. Concentrate on becoming the right woman first.'

2. Nobody's perfect. We cannot expect somebody else to change and become 'right' for us. What we can do is to change ourselves and try and become 'right' for the other person.

38

I Want to Become a Mother

Sayali and Renu both aged ten, were whispering to each other with girlish glee. Sayali's father was a strict man. 'Surely these kids are up to no good,' he thought. 'Always playing with the latest gadgets and wasting time, energy and money. And do they learn anything useful? Nothing! Watching all sorts of things they had no business watching, playing weird games on mobiles – Heavens! What kind of a future were they going to have!'

When Renu left to go home, Sayali came running to her father. 'Papa… we had great fun today.'

'Hmm,' grunted her father. 'What were you and Renu talking about?' he asked.

'I was telling her that I wanted to become a mother. And she told me that she too wanted to become a mother,' said Sayali.

Her father stopped reading his newspaper and yelled at her. 'What nonsense! You should be ashamed of yourself! This is the time when you need to study, not think about becoming a mother. Don't you dare get into bad company and bring the family a bad name!' he cried. He made a mental note to speak to Renu's father about this.

Sayali burst into tears and went crying in search of her mother.

When Renu went home, her father had just come back from work. 'Where had you gone, my dear?' he asked lovingly.

'To Sayali's house,' replied Renu.

'Did you have fun?'

'Yes, we sure did!'

'I hope you have done your homework or else you must do it now,' he said.

'I completed it before I went there, Papa,' said Renu.

'That's like a good girl.' Renu's father was proud of his daughter.

'So, what did you and Sayali play?'

'Papa, Sayali was telling me that she wanted to become a mother. And then, I felt that I should become a mother too.'

Renu's father was a little surprised. 'Why would you and Sayali like to become mothers?' he asked.

'Papa, it's no fun being a child. We must become mothers. Mothers get to decide what we wear, whose birthdays we go to, when we should study, when we should play etc. If we become mothers we will get to decide on our own, isn't it? We wouldn't have to ask our mothers for permission. What fun!'

Renu's father smiled.

Think Tank
---

1. Why did both the fathers react as they did?

The Think Tank encourages you to answer the question on your own before referring to the answer given below.

Answers

1. Sayali's father had preconceived notions about kids and the way they behaved. He thought they were up to no good. He had forgotten that they were growing up, observing, learning and that their thoughts were being shaped accordingly. Due to his preconceived notions, he didn't have the patience to ask Sayali why she wanted to become a mother. He just assumed the worst and reacted accordingly.

   Renu's father had no such preconceived notions about children. He was in fact proud of his daughter. Though surprised that she wanted to become a mother, he had the patience to ask her why. Needless to say, there was no need to overreact.

   Many times we overreact when someone says something because we go by what 'we think they are saying', instead of concentrating on 'what they are saying'.

39

Justice

Munna was a notorious thief. He had begun stealing at a very young age. Once, while trying to steal from a house, the owner caught him. A struggle ensued where Munna tried to get away. But he realized that his opponent was too strong for him. In desperation, Munna stabbed the man with his knife and killed him. He was caught by the police and was tried for murder. But as the evidence was circumstantial, he managed to get away.

As the guards released him, he came across the judge who told him to mend his ways. Munna laughed and told the judge that the law couldn't get the better of him. He told him that though he *had* committed the murder, the law had been unable to prove it.

A few years later, Munna was arrested once more on the charge of murder. The same judge was presiding over his case. Munna pleaded not guilty. However, all the evidence pointed to him and the judge sentenced him to life imprisonment.

As the guards took him away, he once more came across the judge. This time, he pleaded to the judge saying that he was genuinely not guilty and *had not* committed the crime. The judge said that he could do nothing about it. Munna rebuked the law saying that it was unjust that he was being punished for a crime that he had not committed.

The judge said…

Think Tank
---

    1. What did the judge say?

    2. What is the moral of the story?

The Think Tank encourages you to answer these questions on your own before referring to the answers given below.

Answers

1. The judge said, 'It is not the law of the land, but the law of karma at work.'

2. As you sow, so shall you reap. Your deeds will eventually catch up with you. Though the law of the land had been unable to punish Munna the first time, the law of karma had ensured that justice was served.

40

Count Your Blessings

Srinivasan was a very pious man. He owned a huge farm with many animals. Many labourers worked on his farm. His family depended on the income from the farm for their livelihood. One year, they had a wonderful harvest and he earned a lot of money that year. He went to meet his Swamiji and said, 'Swamiji, I have earned a lot of money this year. I would like to make a donation to your ashram.'

The wise Swami answered, 'Son, I have all I need. Don't give me any donation. Just thank God.' Srinivasan humbly accepted Swamiji's advice and expressed his gratitude to God.

The next year, there was a huge flood. He lost almost everything he owned in the flood. It destroyed all his crops. He also lost most of his animals. Some of his labourers also lost their lives. His family was left with barely enough to sustain themselves.

He was truly devastated. He took his family to Swamiji's ashram and told him of what had befallen him. He asked Swamiji what he should do to overcome this situation.

To Srinivasan's surprise, Swamiji said, 'Son, you have all you need. Don't worry about anything. Just thank God.'

―――――――――――――― **Think Tank** ――――――――

1. Why did Swamiji ask Srinivasan to thank God when he had suffered such a huge loss?

―――――――――――――――――――――――――――――――――

The Think Tank encourages you to answer the question on your own before referring to the answer given below.

Answer

1. One must be thankful for one's blessings even in times of suffering. When Swamiji told Srinivasan to thank God, Srinivasan realized that he had a lot to be thankful for. He and his family were alive, safe and together. They were still healthy and could work hard to earn their living again. Contrary to what he had believed, all was not lost.

41

The Secret of Success

Angela was 40. Her husband had just expired some months ago and she had two children to look after. She was able to carry on financially for a month or two, but then, her savings began to dwindle. Soon, the flat owner began demanding outstanding rent payments and so did the other people she had borrowed money from. She realized she was facing poverty and had to take up a job immediately.

She had done a typing and shorthand course years ago, but after her marriage she had never worked. Even though they hadn't been very well off at the time, she had not been able to work as she had had to look after her children.

As days went by, Angela began to look for a job desperately. She went through all the advertisements big and small. She rang up people, went to offices directly and also spoke to friends and relatives, but to no avail. No one wanted an employee who was 40 and had no work experience. With her qualifications, she could only work as an assistant or secretary and all the candidates for such positions were young and trained in secretarial work.

One day, her cousin told her that he knew of a company where the Managing Director (MD), required a secretary. However, he was rumoured to be a slave driver and very difficult to work with. Angela, by this time was truly desperate. She borrowed money for the bus fare and went to the company for the interview.

The Human Resource Manager who was fed up trying to find a 'capable' secretary for the MD eyed Angela warily. Candidate after candidate had been rejected within moments of the interview with the MD and the two candidates who had been selected and had joined, had both been asked to leave within days. None of the other secretarial staff from the company was willing to work with the MD either. He seriously wondered how Angela would be selected for the job.

However, as there was no candidate in sight, he sent her for the interview. The MD asked her about her background and told her that he expected her to be at the top of her work at all times, and that she had to be the last word in efficiency. Angela only nodded and started work that day itself.

As soon as the other secretaries came to know of her appointment, they began gossiping. Some told her tales of the MD. One of them even told her that she might find herself thrown out of the office any day for no rhyme or reason.

Angela worked as the MD's secretary for the next 15 years till he retired, but not before he had her promoted as the Vice President – Administration.

Among the colleagues who came to congratulate her were some of the earlier secretaries who were still working with the company. One of them asked her the one reason she was able to work with such a demanding boss like the MD.

Think Tank

1. What was the reason Angela gave?

2. What is the implication of the story?

The Think Tank encourages you to answer these questions on your own before referring to the answers given below.

Answers

1. Angela's one word answer was 'Poverty'.

2. When we are truly desperate to achieve a goal, we don't notice the problems or obstacles that come our way. We try to find a way around it to reach the goal. Angela was facing poverty. She knew that she needed to hold on to her job for her family's sake. She didn't let things like too much work or an irritable boss bother her, unlike the other secretaries. She ignored all the gossip about the MD and focused only on her work to make ends meet. Once she got used to working hard, she was able to meet the MD's expectations.

42

The Big Bully

Sanket was the leader among his friends at school and had an answer to most of their problems.

One day, he came to know that two of the boys from his group had been beaten up by Manoj, a boy who was quite older to them. Tall and hefty, Manoj had his own group and they were known for bullying boys who were younger and weaker than them.

This made the other boys from Sanket's group very angry. They all decided to go as a team and face Manoj and his group. Sanket was completely against this. He told them that he would go alone. But none of them listened to him. In the end, they all went without him to tackle Manoj and his group after school.

Needless to say, there was a huge fight and the members of both groups were hurt. But Manoj's group finally won the fight. 'Get lost, all of you, and send that puny leader of yours to meet me!' he bellowed.

Sanket had known this would happen. He told his group that this time, he would go alone. Despite their protests, he went alone to meet Manoj and his friends.

They were waiting for him, armed with hockey sticks. They were surprised to see that he was alone and wasn't even armed. They sniggered, 'What a fool he is to come alone.'

As he approached, Manoj's group raised their sticks to hit Sanket. However, he raised one hand confidently and said, 'Wait! I want to speak to your leader.' Now, this confused the group and they expectantly looked at Manoj for guidance.

Sanket was now in front of Manoj. 'What do you want?' asked Manoj rudely.

Sanket raised his face, looked confidently into Manoj's eyes and replied with a smile…

That was the first time anybody had seen tears in Manoj's eyes.

Think Tank

1. What did Sanket say?

2. Why did Manoj cry?

The Think Tank encourages you to answer these questions on your own before referring to the answers given below.

Answers

1. Sanket replied, 'Manoj, I want to be your friend.'

2. Most bullies operate from an inferiority complex. Manoj was doing all this to get attention. By asking Manoj to be his friend, Sanket expressed respect towards him. Manoj had never received respect from anyone before and this moved him to tears.

43

The Slap

Sonalika had lost her elder son three days ago in an accident. The whole family had gathered together. They were waiting for her husband who was an Army officer to return home. Her mother had spoken to him on the phone with a heavy heart. But Sonalika hadn't spoken to him. She hadn't spoken to anyone. Nor had she cried. She sat stunned in shock. She hadn't even attended to her ten-month-old son since the last three days.

All the ladies in the family commented, 'She is in shock. Somebody must bring her out of it. She must be made to cry.'

But Sonalika didn't cry. When her husband stood in the doorway, she didn't even look at him. Her mother went to the door and brought him into the house. He put down his bags and strode across to where Sonalika was sitting on the floor. He caught her by her arms and got her to stand up. Then, to everyone's shock he gave her one tight slap across the face.

Her mother heaved a sigh of relief.

Think Tank

1. Why did Sonalika's husband slap her?

The Think Tank encourages you to answer the question on your own before referring to the answer given below.

Answer

1. Just like it is necessary to express happiness, it is also important to express sorrow. Sonalika had gone into shock on her son's death. Her husband knew that for her well-being, she had to cry and express her pain and sorrow. When he slapped her, she began to cry.

44

Giving Advice

Sharath had just landed a new job at a multinational company. He was very pleased with himself. He and two of his classmates had been chosen by the company from among 60 students from his batch. Due to this, his confidence was at an all-time high.

After he started work, he began dating a girl from his office. They would spend a lot of time together. He told his parents about her and also arranged that she would come home to meet them.

His parents were not pleased on meeting the girl. They both easily saw that she was not the right person for Sharath. His father was very displeased with his choice and made it very clear that if he went ahead to marry the girl, he would have to forget about having his blessings. Sharath then went to his mother. She just smiled and said, 'I am not in favour of this match. But I am with you, my son.'

His father was stunned. He knew his wife had not thought the girl suitable too. Then why was she supporting Sharath? To this, his wife only said, 'Patience.'

As days progressed, Sharath began to treat his mother as his confidante. His father remained aloof. One day, he again asked his wife to convey to Sharath that the girl was not suitable to him. He was bound to get hurt. Again she said, 'Patience.'

A month later, Sharath came home and told his mother that it was all over. The girl's parents had fixed her marriage to someone else and she had decided to marry him rather than face her parents' wrath.

Sharath's mother was a tower of strength to him. Soon, with her help he was able to get over the episode. Later, Sharath's father asked his wife, 'How could you be calm and watch your son be hurt by that girl? You didn't even try to tell him that he was wrong.'

To this, Sharath's mother answered...

Think Tank

1. What did Sharath's mother say?

2. What is the implication of this story?

The Think Tank encourages you to answer these questions on your own before referring to the answers given below.

Answers

1. She said, 'Give advice only if a person is ready to hear it.'

2. Sharath's mother knew that if she too expressed her opposition, Sharath would only see their opposition for the girl and not realize the truth. He was not ready to hear the truth at that time. By telling him, 'I am with you', she assured her son that she would support him no matter what. In due course, he himself realized what his parents wanted to tell him.

45

Shivaji Maharaj and the Dal Rice

This is the story of the time when Shivaji *Maharaj* had escaped from Agra. He disguised himself as a sadhu and began to travel back to his kingdom. When he reached his kingdom after travelling for a long time, he stopped at a village. Exhausted, he looked around to see if he could get food anywhere.

He saw a house nearby and went there to ask for food. The lady of the house came out and asked him to wait for some time while she served the food. Since he was disguised as a sadhu, she didn't recognize him.

After some time, she brought him dal rice. She had placed the rice in a heap on a banana leaf. A banana leaf is flat and has no boundary, unlike a plate. So, when Shivaji *Maharaj* poured the dal over the heap of rice, it flowed over the rice and spilt out of the banana leaf.

The woman looked at him and said, 'How like Shivaji *Maharaj* you are! Make a boundary for the dal so that it won't spill over.'

Think Tank

1. What did the woman mean?

The Think Tank encourages you to answer the question on your own before referring to the answer given below.

Answer

1. No kingdom is safe without a boundary. The woman meant that though Shivaji *Maharaj* had built his entire kingdom quite well, he hadn't created a sturdy boundary for it. That is why it was vulnerable to enemy attacks. Sometimes, the most important lessons are learnt from unexpected quarters.

46

The Beginning of Spirituality

Pritam was the young CEO of a huge company. Having achieved pretty much everything that he had wanted, he had now turned to spirituality. While he read a lot on the subject, he realized that it wasn't enough. He had to learn from a guru. He asked his assistant to find him such a guru.

After a long search, the assistant found such a guru. Busy in his daily schedule, Pritam asked the assistant to contact the guru, specify his requirement and ask the guru to come and meet him. The assistant thought it improper that someone enlightened like the guru be asked to come and see a would-be disciple. But Pritam assured him that he would make the guru very welcome and would treat him with all the honour he deserved. It was just that it was inconvenient to go to the guru, otherwise, he would have gone himself.

So the assistant went to request the guru to come and meet Pritam. The guru said, 'If your boss is truly interested in spirituality, then he has to come to my humble hut and learn.'

The assistant conveyed this message to Pritam. Pritam went to the guru's home. He waited outside the hut while his assistant informed the guru of his arrival. Used to the corporate culture, he thought the guru or his students would come to receive him. But instead, he was asked to go inside the hut.

The height of the door was so short that Pritam had to bend down to get in through the door. There was also no light in the first room. Groping, he made his way to the next room, where he found the guru.

The guru received him and accepted him as his pupil. Pritam was overjoyed. He said, 'I hope you have not been offended by my asking you to come to meet me, O Holy One!'

Think Tank

1. What did the guru say?

The Think Tank encourages you to answer the question on your own before referring to the answer given below.

Answer

1. The guru said, 'I am not offended at all. In fact, I have already taught you the first lesson of spirituality. By coming here, you have put aside your ego of being a CEO. By bending your head, you have learnt to honour others and by finding your way in the darkness, you have come to appreciate light.'

47

The Secret of a Blissful Marriage

Sohan's parents were looking for a bride for him. At times, he wondered how his relationship with his wife would be. His brother who was an astrologer led a happy married life. His wife was always cheerful and content and supported her husband's choice of profession.

One day, someone suggested a girl for Sohan. He took her horoscope and went to consult his brother to see if they matched.

His brother said that they did match and that he should go ahead and meet the girl. But that answer did not satisfy Sohan. '*Bhaiyya*, tell me, will I have a happy married life?' he asked.

His brother said, 'I don't see any problems in your married life in your horoscope.' But even then, Sohan was not satisfied.

He went on further, 'No *Bhaiyya*, I want you to see and tell me if my married life will be as happy as yours.'

His brother looked him in the eye and said...

Think Tank
---

1. What was his brother's reply?

2. What is the implication of this story?

The Think Tank encourages you to answer these questions on your own before referring to the answers given below.

Answers

1. His brother said, 'It will be, only if you work towards it daily.'

2. Stars or planets cannot be held responsible for our success, failure, happiness or sorrow. If we want to be happy or successful at something, be it a job, marriage or a relationship, we have to work towards it daily.

48

Bhaag Lo, Bhaag Lo

A man once went to see his mentor for advice. The mentor asked him the problem. The man said that there was a strong rumour that religious clashes would break out in the area of his residence. Although the police had assured the residents of protection, nobody was sure what would happen. The man was worried about his family's safety. 'What should I do, Sir?' he asked.

'Can you see any way in which you can contribute to solving the problem?' asked the mentor.

'No, I can't,' said the man.

The mentor answered, *'Phir, bhaag lo.'*

Six months later, the man came back to the mentor for advice. This time he said that there had been an outbreak of swine flu in his area and many people were being admitted to hospitals. There was pandemonium. 'What should I do, Sir?' asked the man worried.

'Can you see any way in which you can contribute to solving the problem?' asked the mentor.

'Yes, I can,' said the man. 'I can help create awareness, I can gather my friends to help the patients and their families, I can donate money to help people buy medicines… I can do a lot of things.'

The mentor answered, *'Phir, bhaag lo.'*

When the man had left, the mentor's assistant asked him, 'Sir, why did you advise the man to run away in both situations, especially in the second situation, when he said he could help solve the problem?'

Think Tank

1. What was the mentor's answer?

The Think Tank encourages you to answer the question on your own before referring to the answer given below.

Answer

1. The mentor said that the first time, he had indeed told the man to run away (*Bhaag lo*), because there was nothing that he could do to help solve the problem. But, the second time, when he said, *'Bhaag lo'*, he had asked the man to participate and not run away because he could take firm steps to solve the problem.

49

Objectivity in Relationships

Govind's parents had gone through a bitter divorce six months ago. He was now five-years-old and lived with his father. One day, while he was crossing the road to get to the school bus, a car rammed into him. He fell down unconscious and began to bleed profusely. The school authorities took him to a hospital and informed his father and mother.

Both of them rushed to the hospital when they heard the news. While his father was shocked at the incident, he was also shocked to find that his ex-wife had also been informed of the incident. He created a big ruckus in the hospital, asking the school authorities how they dared inform her, when he was his son's legal guardian. The school authorities told him that they weren't even aware that Govind's parents were divorced. The doctor came and reprimanded him for creating a scene. Only then did he quieten down. Govind's mother stood quietly in a corner.

Sometime later, the doctor came and told them that Govind urgently needed blood. His mother immediately came forward, but she stopped with his father's stern glance. 'You are dead for my son,' he said. He immediately offered to donate his blood.

But the doctor told him that it didn't match Govind's. He then asked, 'Where is the boy's mother? Let's ask her to donate blood. If yours doesn't match, hers will.' Again Govind's mother came ahead and his father once again glared at her and said, 'Keep away from my son. We are divorced and have nothing to do with each other now.'

By now the doctor had completely lost patience with Govind's father. He spoke a few words which finally brought him to his senses.

Think Tank

1. What did the doctor say?

The Think Tank encourages you to answer the question on your own before referring to the answer given below.

Answer

1. The doctor said, 'Look at the relationship objectively. We haven't asked your ex-wife to donate blood; we have asked the child's mother.'

50

A Final Glimpse

Swati's grandmother was dying. She and her younger brother sat by *dadi's* bedside, waiting for her to regain consciousness. Once, when *dadi* woke up, she stared into Swati's face and asked her when Diwali was. Swati replied that it was just two-three days away. *Dadi* then asked her when Prakash would be home and went back to sleep. Prakash was Swati's elder brother who lived in the US. He was to come to India for Diwali.

Swati had informed him of *dadi's* condition and he had promised to get back home as soon as possible. But the way things were, Swati doubted that he would be able to reach before or even during Diwali.

Their parents had died when they were very young and *dadi* had brought them up. She was a woman with tremendous willpower. Prakash was her favourite grandson. He took up the responsibility of their family as soon as he could and when the opportunity came to go to the US, he took it, thinking that it would considerably improve the family's finances. *Dadi* had encouraged him to go. However, she missed him terribly.

Now, *dadi* was waiting for Diwali… for a final glimpse of Prakash. He had promised her that he would come home for Diwali. She wanted to see him for the last time before she died. But Swati thought it looked impossible. Each day *dadi's* condition worsened.

Prakash called to say that he would probably reach one day after Diwali got over. 'Wait for him, *dadi*,' whispered Swati desperately.

She cast her mind back to all their earlier Diwali's since the time they had lost their parents. Diwali had always been a special occasion at *dadi's* place. Actually, it had been more fun than it had been with her parents. *Dadi* called everybody over for Diwali. The entire family got together and the old and the young of the family made it a point to be there for the occasion. *Dadi* had always made sure that she bought Swati and her brothers at least one set of new clothes. Somehow, Swati never remembered *dadi* buying any new saris for Diwali.

After he started earning, Prakash bought *dadi* her first new sari in a long time. She was extremely happy and had had tears in her eyes. 'I'll get promoted next year and buy you a better one,' he had told her.

And now, Swati just hoped *dadi* would be able to hold on to the thin line of life till Prakash got back... to see him... to see the beautiful sari he would get her.

Diwali came and the entire hospital was decked up with lights, *diyas*, *rangoli* and small lanterns. Along with the other patients, Swati too felt a ray of hope on the first day of Diwali. *Dadi* awoke and remained awake for a while. She looked at the *diyas* and decorations in the room and asked, 'Is it Diwali today? Where is Prakash?'

'Oh, he'll be here soon, *dadi*, what with all the mad rush during the festival season,' answered Swati enthusiastically. *Dadi* only nodded and closed her eyes once again. Then she woke up on the last day of Diwali and once again Swati told her that Prakash would be coming soon. She didn't dare tell her that it was the last day of Diwali.

The day after Diwali, Prakash had still not arrived. He would be able to reach their city only the next day. The nurse who had gone home for Diwali had joined duty. She began to remove the decorations and *diyas* from *dadi's* room.

By now, Swati was desperate. She stopped the nurse and asked her, 'Can you please wait for another day before you remove the decorations and *diyas*?'

The nurse nodded but asked, 'Why?'

Think Tank

1. What was Swati's answer?

The Think Tank encourages you to answer the question on your own before referring to the answer given below.

Answer

1. Swati was worried that if *dadi* awoke and saw that the decorations had been removed, she would know that Diwali was over and Prakash had still not come. She was worried that *dadi* would completely give up hope of seeing him again and would lose her will to live. So she asked the nurse to leave the decorations as they were. As long as her grandmother thought it was Diwali, she would wait for a final glimpse of Prakash who would reach the next day.

51

The Adopted Child

Rhea and her husband had adopted a baby girl a year after their son was born. Of course, the children didn't know about it yet. Rhea knew it was time to tell them, as they were now teenagers. She was a little worried that someone else would tell them before she and her husband did and the children would take it the wrong way.

One day, her worst fears came true. At a function, one of her cousins nastily said to her daughter, 'Of course, you aren't as beautiful as your mother. You are only adopted. Now, your brother is as handsome as his father.'

Rhea's daughter was heartbroken and her son was taken aback. He didn't know that his beloved *Choti* was adopted. He was quite confused as to how to react. Meanwhile, Rhea's daughter was so hurt, she couldn't stop crying.

Rhea knew that the time had come for them to explain the adoption to their children. She knew they must be careful that it didn't shatter her daughter's belief in them and change her son's behaviour towards his sister. It was a tightrope walk.

As she and her husband sat the children down for a talk, her daughter was simply inconsolable. 'Is it true that I am adopted?' she asked her father.

'Yes, *beta*,' he replied.

'Do you know what that Aunty said to me? I am not beautiful like my mother because I am not her daughter. Now people will hate me because of this. Why did you adopt me when you already had a son?' she asked tearfully.

Her father's reply brought a smile to her face.

Think Tank

1. What did her father say?

The Think Tank encourages you to answer the question on your own before referring to the answer given below.

Answer

1. Her father said, 'Our own child was God's gift to us and you are the gift we asked God for.'

52

Have the Drink

Tina's parents were having a party at home. She was excited. There would be tasty snacks, she could wear her best party frock and look stunning in her new sandals. 'She's growing up fast,' thought her mother.

Tina observed that her father and her uncles were having a yellow drink at the party. One of her uncles had become quite talkative after he had had quite a bit of it. The ladies however, didn't seem to be drinking it; nor were the children. Her curiosity was aroused. 'I must taste it,' she thought.

The day after the party, she found a huge bottle of the yellow drink in the fridge. She was excited. 'Mummy, what is this yellow bottle?' she asked.

'That's not for you, dear. It belongs to your father.'

Tina turned to him. 'Papa, I want to taste that yellow stuff. I saw all of you drinking it yesterday.'

Her father was aghast. 'It's not for you. Did you see your mother or your friends drinking it?'

Tina thought and said, 'No. But I want to drink it.' Her father refused and this led to a lot of arguments till dinner. Finally, when

Tina resorted to tears before her helpless father, her mother said, 'Okay, Tina. You can have the drink.'

As her father watched shocked, Tina gave her best smile.

'Why did you agree?' Tina's father angrily asked her mother.

'Wait and watch,' she said.

Think Tank

1. Why did Tina's mother agree to give her the yellow drink?

2. What happened when Tina had the drink?

The Think Tank encourages you to answer these questions on your own before referring to the answers given below.

Answers

1) and 2) Tina took a sip of the drink and spat it out. She poured the rest of the glass in the sink. Tina's mother knew what her reaction would be and that is why she agreed to give her the drink. Once Tina's curiosity was satisfied, she was no longer interested in the drink. She would never ask for it again. But had they refused to let her have it, she would have been all the more attracted to it.

53

A Different Answer

Once, a guru decided to test his pupils. He gave each one of them a banana and asked them to eat it where absolutely no one could watch them.

All the pupils went far and wide to eat the fruit. One of them hid in a room, another went far into the fields, yet another went underground etc. They all came back having eaten their bananas.

Only one pupil came back without eating the banana. The guru asked him, 'Did you not find a single place where no one was watching you, my son?'

The pupil's answer told the guru that he was different from the others.

Think Tank

---

1. What was the pupil's reply?

The Think Tank encourages you to answer the question on your own before referring to the answer given below.

Answer

1. The pupil replied, '*Guruji*, everywhere I went, I found my own eyes watching me. So, I couldn't eat the banana.'

54

The Blind Tutor

Sushant had lost his sight in an accident. His parents were beside themselves with worry. The doctors had told them that he would never be able to see again.

Sushant suddenly found that he couldn't move without someone's help. It was very frustrating for the little boy who was only eight. In one stroke, the pace of his hectic life had come to a standstill. Life had suddenly snatched away everything he had – school, friends, play, studies, opportunities... everything. He soon lost interest in living. Then his father heard about Aryaji.

Aryaji was a blind scholar who taught blind students. He had set up a school for them. He taught them everything, right from coping with the day-to-day world, their tasks and their studies. Sushant's father requested Aryaji to accept Sushant as his student and bring back his interest in life.

Aryaji told Sushant's father that he would come to meet Sushant at his home the next day. Sushant's father asked him if he should come to escort him to his house. But Aryaji only smiled.

The next day, Aryaji came to meet Sushant at the appointed time. The boy sat staring ahead with a blank look. 'To be blind is not to be helpless, my child,' said Aryaji. 'Even the sighted are found lacking in vision. Many of them are not able to see what a blind person can. Clear thinking, logical deduction and the sense of sound are as important as sight. Once you learn to make use of them, you can function like a normal person.'

'How can it be?' asked Sushant puzzled. Just then, his mother came in and said, 'First, have something to eat. I have made *ghavan* (a dish similar to *dosas* or rice pancakes).'

Aryaji said to Sushant, 'Now, if I tell you how many *ghavans* your mother has made, will you believe me that one need not see and can still function normally?'

'Yes,' said Sushant.

Aryaji correctly told Sushant the number of *ghavans* his mother had made. Sushant was intrigued. 'How did you know, without being able to see?' he asked.

Think Tank

1. How did Aryaji know how many *ghavans* Sushant's mother had made?

The Think Tank encourages you to answer the question on your own before referring to the answer given below.

Answer

1. When the batter of *ghavans* is spread on the *tava* (pan), it makes a distinct 'chrrr' sound. Aryaji could not see, but he made use of his sense of hearing to know what his eyes couldn't tell him.

55

Merry Christmas!

Christmas that year was not a happy one for Thomas. It was the first Christmas without his wife. She had died, leaving him and their four-year-old daughter, Lavina. The very thought of Christmas without his wife was unbearable for Thomas. On top of that, he had lost his job too.

He was drowned in his grief and sorrow. Lavina, on her part, kept pestering her father with numerous questions and Thomas couldn't answer them. After some time, he began to avoid her altogether.

His mother came to stay with them for Christmas. She arranged for a Christmas tree, much to Lavina's joy.

On Christmas Day, Lavina cheerfully went to wish her father Merry Christmas. Her father only grunted. She gave him a box wrapped with golden paper and said, 'This is your Christmas gift, Papa.'

Thomas was infuriated. Had Lavina taken money from his mother to buy him a gift? he wondered. Nevertheless, he smiled and took the box from her hand. He opened it, only to find that it was empty.

He then lost his temper. 'Do you think it's April Fools' Day? Giving me an empty box as a Christmas present!'

With tears in her eyes, Lavina said...

Think Tank

1. What was in the box?

2. What is the moral of the story?

The Think Tank encourages you to answer these questions on your own before referring to the answers given below.

Answers

1. Lavina said, 'The box is not empty, Papa. I have put all my love into it.'

2. We do not see the blessings that we have and only grieve for what we have lost. Thomas had a daughter who loved him unconditionally. But he ignored her love and was caught up grieving for his wife whom he had lost.

56

Athithi Devo Bhava

Shambhu was on the way to his mother's village. Since he didn't know anyone there, his mother had told him to meet Ramlal, her brother's friend who lived in the village, in case Shambhu needed to stay the night.

Shambhu finished his work in the evening and decided that he would have to stay at Ramlal's house. When he reached his house, Ramlal welcomed him. Ramlal's house was barely more than a hut. They were sitting in the light of the lantern. After sometime, Ramlal's wife brought Shambhu a plate filled with vegetables, dal, rice and chapatis. Then Ramlal did something quite surprising. He blew out the flame from the lantern and said to Shambhu, 'I hope you don't require the light while eating.' Shambhu said nothing.

Then Ramlal's wife brought him his plate. They began to eat. While the food was delicious, Shambhu was not used to eating without the light and felt quite uncomfortable. However, he said nothing to his host. He could only hear Ramlal as he made noises while eating.

The next day, he left for the city after thanking Ramlal for his hospitality. 'Oh no! You are like a son to me. You are welcome anytime,' said Ramlal. Shambhu returned home.

After a few days, his mother's brother came to meet them. He was surprised when Shambhu told him that he had stayed at Ramlal's house. 'Did you have dinner with him?' he asked Shambhu.

'Yes, the food was very good,' answered Shambhu.

'Did Ramlal eat with you?' asked his uncle.

'Yes, he did. Only, he extinguished the lantern while we were eating. It was very difficult for me to eat in the dark. I don't understand why one would treat a guest that way.'

'Ideally, you shouldn't have gone to Ramlal's house to stay. Didn't you understand why he extinguished the lantern?' asked Shambhu's uncle.

--------------------- **Think Tank** ---------------------

1. Why had Ramlal extinguished the lantern?

_____

The Think Tank encourages you to answer the question on your own before referring to the answer given below.

Answer

1. Ramlal had not wanted his guest to know that he didn't have enough food to eat. That is why he extinguished the lantern while eating. While he let his guest have a full meal, he himself had very little food. Contrary to what Shambhu had thought, Ramlal had followed the principle of *Athithi Devo Bhava* and treated his guest like God.

57

Not Without My Mother

Akanksha's mother was not well. She was 70-years-old and the doctor said she was losing her strength.

Akanksha decided to do all she could for her mother. She worked in a company as a senior accountant. She asked the management for an option to work from home. She worked hard daily doing office work, housework and took care of her mother as well. Yet, she was always smiling and never complained about the hardships she had to face.

Once, her colleagues came to meet her at home. They saw her struggle to complete all her work and how tired she was. One of them asked her, 'You are doing all this for your mother. But what about yourself? What about your personal space, your personal life?'

Think Tank
---

1. What did Akanksha say?

The Think Tank encourages you to answer the question on your own before referring to the answer given below.

Answer

1. Akanksha said, 'My duty is first towards my mother. I owe my life and what I am today to her. Had she not brought me home from an orphanage, I wouldn't have been living the life I am.'

58

The Animals

A teacher was once telling his students, 'There are two animals within all of us. The first is evil and is symbolized by anger, hatred, jealousy, sorrow, ego, guilt etc. The second animal is good, symbolized by love, joy, peace, hope, kindness etc. These two animals are constantly at war with each other.'

A student asked him, 'Which of the animals wins, Sir?'

─────────── **Think Tank** ───────────

1. What was the teacher's reply?

─────────────────────────────

The Think Tank encourages you to answer the question on your own before referring to the answer given below.

Answer

1. The teacher's reply was, 'The one we feed.'

CONFIDENCE
and
STRESS MANAGEMENT

59

Speak Up!

Freedom fighter Bal Gangadhar Tilak or Lokmanya Tilak is known for the roaring challenge he issued to the British regime in his editorial titled, 'Is the government out of its mind?'

Since his childhood, he was well-known for his confidence and outspoken attitude. Once, during his school days, his classmate ate peanuts in the class and threw their shells on the floor. Later, when the teacher came, he saw the shells on the floor and asked the students who was responsible for the act.

When nobody owned up, the teacher decided to punish all the students. He asked them to stand in a row and started hitting them on their palms with a stick. When it was Tilak's turn, the teacher asked him to hold out his hand. But he refused and told the teacher that he would not take the punishment.

--------------------- **Think Tank** ---------------------

1. What was the reason Tilak gave his teacher for not accepting the punishment?

2. Why did the teacher accept it?

3. What can you learn from this story?

The Think Tank encourages you to answer these questions on your own before referring to the answers given below.

Answers

1. Tilak was fearless because he had done nothing wrong. He confidently told the teacher that neither had he eaten the peanuts, nor had he thrown the shells, so he wouldn't take the punishment. His confidence helped him face the situation and convince his teacher that he was not guilty.

2. The teacher appreciated his confidence and realized that he was wrongly punishing Tilak.

3. This childhood incident in Tilak's life is a guiding force for all of us even today. You don't have to accept punishment for the wrongs that you have not done. But in order to do this, like Tilak you must have the confidence and courage to speak up and face any situation that may arise due to this.

60

A Grain of Sand

'I'm the best!' said Hari greatly pleased with himself. He had given a rocking performance that year and had just been promoted to the position of CEO. 'No one, nothing can beat me now!' he exclaimed to the heavens above. 'I've done it all on my own. Nobody can take this credit from me.'

'Yes, my son. But do not be so proud of your achievements. One must be humble. Destiny has a way of helping us towards achieving our goals,' said his mother.

'Your 'destiny' has done nothing for me Mamma. Nothing! I have put in my blood, sweat and tears for each and everything I have achieved till today.' His mother gave him a grave look, but said nothing.

Hari went and stood in his balcony on the 15th floor, facing the sea. No, he thought. His mother was wrong. It was he, himself who had achieved everything. Surely his mother knew that. And no one could defeat him now. Not even you, God! he thought as he looked up to the sky which looked down upon him lovingly.

I am not going to thank you for playing a part in my success. No. Neither did you help me in my success nor can you cause my failure, he thought, his head held high.

As if in answer, there was a gust of wind which blew a grain of sand into his eyes. For the next ten minutes Hari sat, his head bent, trying to remove it.

--------- **Think Tank** ---------

1. What is the lesson to be learnt from this story?

_____

The Think Tank encourages you to answer the question on your own before referring to the answer given below.

Answer

1. No matter what you achieve, always remember that you can never become bigger than the Lord. He always has a role in our lives and everything that we achieve, we achieve through His will. It will take only a single moment for Him to crush our pride.

61

Ignorance is Bliss

Akash was an expert at Science. He read up anything and everything on the subject and constantly questioned his teachers and parents about it.

One day, when they were studying Biology, he came to know an interesting fact about bumblebees. His teacher said that the structure of the bumblebee's body and wings was such that technically speaking, it was impossible for it to fly. But, fly it did!

This intrigued Akash who decided he would search the internet to find out how bumblebees could fly. When he came home, he told his parents and younger brother what he had learnt in school.

'I wonder how the bumblebee can fly if the structure of its body and wings makes it impossible,' said Akash.

His younger brother immediately quipped…

Think Tank

1. What did his younger brother say?

2. What can we learn from this story?

The Think Tank encourages you to answer these questions on your own before referring to the answers given below.

Answers

1. The younger brother said, 'The bumblebee can fly because it doesn't know this.'

2. Our so-called limitations work only when we know about them. If we do not know that a particular limitation exists, it simply doesn't affect us.

62

Stand Tall!

Laxmi was very tall for her age. When she entered her teens, her mother took her to a doctor to ask him if there was a problem and how much taller she was going to become.

Of course, Laxmi's confidence took a huge beating due to this. Additionally, her parents moved to another city where she had to adjust to new schoolmates as well. Towering over everybody else, she soon earned the nickname of 'Skyscraper'. To avoid this, she tended to slouch. But her class teacher would admonish her by saying, 'Stand up straight, child! Hold your head high!'

Once, during their Personality Development class, their class teacher asked everyone what their ambition was. When she asked Laxmi, everyone laughed. Someone said, 'She wants to be a skyscraper.' Laxmi cringed and tears welled up in her eyes.

The class teacher looked at the entire class for one full minute and said, 'I'll tell you what Laxmi's ambition is. Laxmi's ambition is to be...'

On hearing the teacher's words, the students were awestruck. Laxmi wiped her tears and stood up to her full height, holding her head high...

—————————— **Think Tank** ——————————

1. What did the teacher say?

_____

The Think Tank encourages you to answer the question on your own before referring to the answer given below.

Answer

1. The teacher told everybody that Laxmi would become a supermodel. She went on to say that taller women carried clothes beautifully and that is why supermodels had to be really tall. By saying so, she made the children realize that there was nothing wrong in being tall. There was no reason to ridicule Laxmi; rather her height would give her an advantage the others did not have.

63

A Little Bottle of Jam

Savita was the wife of a rich businessman. She was very caring and made sure that everyone who came to their house was looked after well and properly served the food they liked. She also believed in helping the poor and gave away either food or money to them. She had also taught her young daughter the same. She was also a very good cook and made various kinds of jams according to the seasons. These were very popular among her friends and relatives.

But after some years, they fell on hard times. Her husband had to shut down his business. They had to sell their bungalow and shift into a much smaller house. Her husband began to work at a small company. They depended entirely on his weekly wages. They also had to wear cast-offs and live very frugally. Yet, Savita maintained her pleasant attitude.

One day, Savita was waiting for her husband to come back. With the wages he would bring, she would buy vegetables for the next week. Today, they would have to sustain on that last bottle of jam that they had.

On that very day, her daughter came back from school and said that they were collecting money and food for the poor and each child had been asked to bring something as his/her contribution.

Savita was aghast. She was filled with anger at herself that she had nothing to give her daughter. 'Is there anybody who is poorer than we are?' she cried. 'Today, I have nothing to give to the poor because I myself am one of them! Let my daughter realize today that we have nothing to give anybody.'

'Keep your voice down,' said her mother-in-law. 'Give your daughter the last bottle of jam to take as her contribution to the poor.'

Think Tank

1. Why did Savita's mother-in-law say so?

The Think Tank encourages you to answer the question on your own before referring to the answer given below.

Answer

1. All her life, Savita's daughter had been taught that she had to do her bit for society. If at this stage, Savita would have told her that they were too poor to help anybody, that impression would have stuck with the child forever. It would have affected her confidence and belief that she could be of help to others. Savita's mother-in-law wanted the child to always feel that she was a part of the solution and not a part of the problem.

64

The Lucky Coin

Once a general and his army were on the way to a battle. They knew that they had few chances of victory. To instil courage in the soldiers, the general told them to arrange for a prayer meeting where they would pray for success. After the prayer, the General said, 'I am now going to flip my lucky coin. Heads we win, tails we lose.' He flipped the coin and it was heads. 'Great,' said the General. 'Now there's no way we can lose. This is my lucky coin. If it says we win, we win.'

The spirits of the soldiers rose. They fought courageously and won the battle.

After their victory, the soldiers arranged for a celebration. While celebrating, one of the soldiers said, 'It's true, Sir. Victory depends on fate.'

'No. Victory depends on how bravely and strategically you fight in the war,' said the General.

'No doubt we fought bravely, Sir,' continued the soldier. 'But we also had the support of fate, didn't we. The flipping of the lucky coin and it resting at 'heads' was a matter of fate, wasn't it?'

The General smiled, took out his lucky coin from his pocket and showed it to the soldier. The soldier's eyes widened with shock.

—————————————— **Think Tank** ——————————————

1. What was so shocking about the coin?

2. What is the implication of this story?

_____

The Think Tank encourages you to answer these questions on your own before referring to the answers given below.

Answers

1. The coin that the general showed the soldier had heads on both the sides.

2. We may happily put down our victory or defeat to fate but actually, success or failure depends on our efforts and the way we fight our battles. The general had flipped the coin simply to put his soldiers' minds at ease and help them win the battle. There was nothing lucky about the coin.

65

Choose What You Believe

Niranjan was born with a deformity in his legs. He had very little strength in them. The doctor said that it would be a miracle if Niranjan walked. His grandmother wanted him to become a wrestler like his grandfather. It had been his last wish. But here, the doctor was saying it was impossible.

She asked the doctor what would help to cure Niranjan. The doctor said that there was no cure as such. At the most, she could massage his legs daily with a medicated oil which he prescribed. But he wasn't sure how much it would help.

Niranjan's grandmother massaged his legs twice a day for one hour at a time. She also asked the village priest who told her of some mantras which would help in his recovery. She also observed a fast for him to recover.

When Niranjan turned three, he was finally able to walk. For almost a year, he could only walk by holding onto something. His grandmother would hold both his hands and help him to walk. By the age of five, he was walking with crutches.

When he turned six, his grandmother went to meet one of the wrestlers in the village. She wanted Niranjan to become a wrestler. The wrestler laughed. He said, 'Even healthy boys find it difficult to take up this profession and stick to it. What will your child do? How will he cope? Your husband was a master. But not everyone can follow in his shoes. Forget it.'

'I know he can become as good a wrestler as his grandfather,' said Niranjan's grandmother. 'Can't you even give him a chance to try?' she asked. 'Alright,' said the wrestler. 'The day you get him to run around the whole village, I will teach him.'

It took Niranjan almost two years to accomplish this feat. The wrestler gave in and began to train Niranjan. Life was an even more difficult struggle for him. Everyone, the other wrestlers, champions, and his fellow students said he would never succeed.

But Niranjan and his grandmother never let go of their never say die spirit. Gradually, he improved his technique, his strength and skills and became one of the better wrestlers in the village. From good to great was another great struggle. But he did accomplish it. Later, he also went on to win the Hind Kesari Award.

When he was asked how he came up against all odds, he said, 'My grandmother gave me a mantra. I just used it.'

--------- **Think Tank** ---------

1. What was the mantra that Niranjan's grandmother gave him?

The Think Tank encourages you to answer the question on your own before referring to the answer given below.

Answer

1. Niranjan's grandmother knew that most people he would meet would tell him that he wouldn't succeed. The mantra she gave him was, 'When somebody tells you that you can't do something, believe that it means that you can!'

66

Be Yourself

A man was watering the plants in his terrace garden. The flowers in bloom gladdened his heart.

However, a few days later he found that the flowers of all the plants had suddenly wilted and one or two buds had not even bloomed.

He asked them what had happened and why they had wilted. The lily said that it was bored with itself because it was not as bright as the marigold. The marigold was upset with itself because it didn't smell like the jasmine. The jasmine was jealous that in spite of its lovely smell it wasn't as popular as the rose.

Only the cactus looked happy and it also had a small flower which had bloomed that day. 'How come you are happy, dear Cactus, when the rest, in spite of being more beautiful than you are sad?' asked the man.

Think Tank

1. What did the cactus say?

2. What is the implication of this story?

The Think Tank encourages you to answer these questions on your own before referring to the answers given below.

Answers

1. The cactus said, 'I am happy as I am, because I know I am here because you want me to be. My joy is in surviving and doing my best.'

2. Each one of us is unique. Nor is there anyone like us, nor can we be like others. So, we shouldn't compare ourselves with them. We must learn to be ourselves and accept ourselves as we are.

67

The False Belief

A father and son were passing by some elephants and their mahouts in the jungle. The son noticed that each elephant was bound to a peg by a small rope tied to its leg. The rope was too small compared to the elephant's size. The son wondered why the elephants who could easily break the miniscule rope and get away, did not attempt to do so.

He asked his father the reason. The father said, 'They are similar to us humans. It's a matter of belief.'

────────────── **Think Tank** ──────────────

1. What did the father mean?

2. How were elephants similar to humans?

───

The Think Tank encourages you to answer these questions on your own before referring to the answers given below.

Answers

1. When elephants are very young, their mahouts use a rope to bind them to the peg. Since they are young, they cannot break free from that rope and as time passes, they slowly come to believe that they cannot break away and thus, they give up even trying.

2. In reality, adult elephants can break away from the rope at any time. But because they have tried and failed earlier, they are stuck to their false belief and give up trying to break free. It is the same with humans.

68

'I Can't Do It!'

A man bought a flashy new car. He parked it next to his old car which was a very old model that had belonged to his father. He couldn't bear to part with it for sentimental reasons.

The new car was very proud of its looks and speed. It ignored the old car at first. Then, after a few days, it felt sorry for the old car, as its owner did not take it out anymore. Then it began to talk to the old car. 'How many years have you been running?' it asked.

'Almost twenty years now,' said the old car. The new car was surprised to hear this. It asked the old car, 'Where did your master take you?'

The old car said, 'He was in the ministry, so he travelled all over the state, through various big and small districts and villages too. Be it rain or shine, he had to travel a lot.'

The new car was shocked. It asked the old car, 'And where does my master work? Does he have to travel a lot, too?'

The old car replied, 'He too works in the ministry. Yes, he too has to travel.'

That was it! The next day, the new car refused to start. The owner called the mechanic who said there seemed to be nothing wrong with the new car. The old car asked the new car, 'What's wrong, son?'

The new car replied, 'I was just thinking of the number of kilometres that you must have travelled all those years and the various terrains you must have gone over, and the various seasons you must have run in. I don't think I can do it. I am so stressed, I cannot move.'

'You can do it, my son,' said the old car kindly.

'But all those kilometres?' asked the new car.

The old car quietly looked at the new car and said...

The new car heaved a sigh of relief and smiled.

Think Tank

1. What did the old car say?

2. What is the implication of this story?

The Think Tank encourages you to answer these questions on your own before referring to the answers given below.

Answers

1. The old car said, 'You don't have to run all those kilometres at once. Take it one step at a time. Each step will lead you to a further step and you will accomplish your life's journey.'

2. Most of us get bogged down by the work that we have to do and all the things we have to accomplish. But if we just break down the task to the next moment or the next day, the same mammoth task becomes achievable and we can complete our journey.

69

The Magic Tree

Everyone went to the wise old uncle in their building when they needed help or advice. He was always able to solve their problems with his wisdom.

Kishor was completely stressed! Today had been the worst. It seemed like his boss, colleagues and vendors together had decided to give him a heart attack! To add to his problems, his family too had complained that he never had time for them. Hell! He never had breathing space for himself!

He went to uncle and expressed his woes. 'I am fed up, Uncle. I want to end it all. But I must live. And I can't go on this way. I need a solution. Any more stress and I shall explode!' Uncle looked at him calmly.

'There is a way to reduce your stress. But you will have to do as I say,' said Uncle.

'Anything,' replied Kishor.

'There is a hill near our building. If you go up the hill, you will find a huge tree. It's a magic tree. Sit under that tree for ten minutes daily. Do this for a month. You will be relieved of your stress. But there is one condition. You should leave your wallet, mobile phone and watch at home. Otherwise, the tree's magic won't work,' he said. Kishor agreed.

As expected, after a month, Kishor came to meet uncle, his face fresh and radiant. 'Thank you very much Uncle, for introducing me to the Magic Tree.'

Think Tank

1. What was the magic that the tree had performed?

The Think Tank encourages you to answer the question on your own before referring to the answer given below.

Answer

1. The tree was not magical. Uncle had only brought Kishor close to nature. When Kishor went to the tree, he was away from his mobile phone, wallet, watch and everything else that claimed his time. His time, when he was with the tree was his own. With no interruptions, he began watching the sunset, feeling the evening wind in his face and breathing the fresh air on the hill. The climb up the hill also did him a world of good. Slowly, the time he spent with the tree each day gradually increased and so did his time with himself. This reduced his stress and tension.

70

In the End...

After a tough game, all the chess pieces sat in their box talking about how the game had been. 'I was so stressed out!' said the white Bishop. 'Goodness! I had to be so careful of each step I took.'

'That's nothing compared to the stress I was in,' said the black Queen. 'Such a tough game with most of our pawns gone and additionally, I was also responsible for the King's safety.'

'That's no big deal,' said the black King. 'I was more stressed out throughout the game as compared to all of you. I am responsible for everything that happens and one wrong move and the game is over!'

'That's right! We kings are the most stressed among all of you,' confirmed the white King.

The black rook who was with them had said nothing as yet.

'Weren't you stressed out by the game, Rook?' asked everyone else.

'No, rather I enjoyed it. I had a great time. I always do,' he said.

'How come you enjoy each game and aren't stressed? After all, you lost!' said the white King nastily.

'I enjoy each game because, for me, there is only one outcome of every game,' the Rook said.

Think Tank

1. What, according to the Rook was the outcome of every game?

2. What is the moral of this story?

The Think Tank encourages you to answer these questions on your own before referring to the answers given below.

Answers

1. The Rook said, 'No matter what our roles, after every game, we all end up in the same box.'

2. Throughout our lives, we get stressed with various so-called positive or negative outcomes. This spoils our chances of enjoying the game of life and giving it our all. But we need to realize that it is the only time we have. At the end of it all, no matter how important our role, we shall all go back to the same place. Thus, we should live, enjoy and play the game of life to the best of our ability without getting stressed by outcomes.

HUMAN EMOTIONS

71

The Will to Live

Shankar slowly gained consciousness. Through his half-open eyelids he could make out a shape next to him. It belonged to a huge, middle aged, surly-looking woman. Have I reached hell?, he thought. 'Where am I?' he asked.

'Hospital,' she replied sourly. 'You must thank your stars you're alive.'

'Alive?? Am I alive?' He groaned, holding his head in his hands. 'But I wanted to end it all. I wanted to get it over with. Why am I alive?'

'It's time for your medicine,' she said coolly.

'Why? I don't need it,' he protested.

'Oh yes, you do. You must recover,' she said matter-of-factly.

'But there is no use, no purpose.'

'There is always a purpose,' replied the nurse in a strict voice. 'You only need to find it, and for that you need to be alive. You have absolutely no right to take your life. So take your medicines. Be strong, get up and face the world,' she admonished.

'No. I don't want to live. Who saved me? Why did they? There was no need! No need! No need!' he shouted.

'There is no need to shout,' she said in a voice louder than his. 'Now take your medicines, eat your food and go to bed. I'll see you tomorrow.'

'Don't be so sure. Maybe I will try to suicide once more. Who knows, I may be successful the second time! Maybe, we won't be speaking this way tomorrow,' he said.

'I am sure we will,' said the nurse.

'Oh NO! We won't! I'll finish myself off at midnight.'

'Oh no, you won't,' she said confidently.

'How do you know?' he asked.

'You won't try again,' she said, going out of the room.

Wouldn't try again... Did she mean he didn't have the guts to do it again? How stupid! Hadn't he done it once? Had it not been for the person who had saved him, he would have been out of it all. Despair flooded him until sleep took over.

When he awoke the next morning, the nurse was with him once more. 'You must help me. I want to die,' he beseeched. She said nothing but simply looked at him and went out of the room. The doctor then came and gave him further bad news that he would recover in a matter of two weeks. It was too much for him. He held his hands in his head and cried like a baby.

After the doctor left, the nurse came in with her usual tray of medicines. She took a syringe and gave him an injection. 'What's the use? I told you, I don't want to live,' he remonstrated.

'And I just helped you get out of it all,' she said calmly.

'What do you mean?' he asked, confused.

'You can say your prayers. The injection I have given you will take you away from this world in no time at all. A swift, painless death,' she said assuredly, as he looked at her, his face contorted with horror.

Think Tank

1. Why had the nurse given him the lethal injection?

The Think Tank encourages you to answer the question on your own before referring to the answer given below.

Answer

1. The nurse clearly understood that Shankar did not actually want to die. When he had the choice to live, he did not want to take that choice. Only when she forced death upon him without warning, did he understand how much he wanted to live. The nurse hadn't given him a lethal dose at all. She only told him that she had, to enliven his will to live.

72

A Child's Gift

Money is tight! How hard I have to work, thought Sakshi. After working the whole day, now she had to do the dishes, wash the clothes, cut vegetables for tomorrow… The list was endless. How awful for her daughter, little Sonu. No father to bring her toys, take her for a walk or play with her. Life was tough. But Sakshi was determined to get over her misfortune. She would see that Sonu became a doctor, she thought with pride as she went about her household chores.

She reached for her container of washing powder. But alas, there was so little left. It would wash only a handful of clothes. Sakshi tried to keep her cool. She used a little of the powder and soaked in the few clothes that needed immediate washing. Of course, so did the rest; but they would have to wait.

Just then, Sonu came running in from the playground. 'Mamma, see the gift I've made for you!' Her face was caked with mud and so was her frock. It was one of her better ones. Sakshi threw a fit! 'Goodness, Sonu! How dare you go and play in the mud wearing one of your better dresses? And that too, dirtying it completely? As though I have nothing to do all day! We don't even have enough powder to wash the necessary clothes and you just create even more laundry.'

'But Mamma, Rani called me to play. She was teaching me…' she suddenly broke off as Sakshi slapped her in rage. 'And now, you have also learnt to talk back to me!'

Sonu burst into tears, but Sakshi was having none of it. 'Go and sit in that corner till dinner is ready,' she said.

'But Mamma…'

'Shut up!' scolded Sakshi and Sonu did as she was told.

Sakshi knew it wasn't Sonu's fault that she had played in the mud. All children did. The problem was that Sakshi simply wasn't able to make ends meet. Sonu had borne the brunt of her frustration. But she couldn't go on sheltering Sonu from the harsh realities of their life, she reasoned with herself. She knew she could not afford the time, energy and the money that it required. She was doing all that she could. Still, she had been hard on the child.

'Sonu, come to eat *beta*,' said Sakshi softly. Sonu came slowly, her hands behind her back and nervously stood near her mother. Sakshi sat down on her knees so that she was face-to-face with Sonu. 'I am sorry, *beta*. Will you be a good girl and forgive your Mamma?' she asked. With two sad eyes, Sonu looked at her and nodded.

'Have you really forgiven me, child?' asked Sakshi.

'Yes I have, Mamma.' How forgiving children were, Sakshi thought.

'But now that I have forgiven you, will you see what I have brought you?' asked Sonu.

'Of course I will, darling!' said Sakshi.

Sonu held out her hands and Sakshi's eyes widened with surprise

and a tear slowly rolled down her cheek at the invaluable gift that
Sonu held in her palms.

-------------------- **Think Tank** --------------------

1. What was the gift that Sonu had brought for her
   mother?

2. Why was the gift invaluable?

_The Think Tank encourages you to answer these questions on your
own before referring to the answers given below._

Answers

1. Sonu held in her hand, *laddoos* which she had made out of
   mud. 'This is for you Mamma. Yesterday, you made *laddoos* for
   me, so today, I told Rani to teach me to make *laddoos* for you,'
   she said.

2. The *laddoos* were a symbol of Sonu's thoughtful attitude towards
   her mother. While Sakshi was lamenting that there was no one
   to help her, her daughter was busy thinking of ways to make her
   happy. This gave her hope in their grim situation.

73

A Matter of Routine

'Love comes from doing small things daily,' advised Shobha *masi* to her youngest niece Shruti. 'You don't have to do huge things to show your love. Respect too, is a form of love.'

Shruti's in-laws were coming to stay with them for good. Till then, it had just been she and her husband. She was wondering whether she would get along with her in-laws and be able to live together harmoniously. Till now, their relations had been quite good, but everything always seemed green from far-off.

'But what if I don't get along with them and want them to leave?' asked a worried Shruti.

'It is not possible for a person to always get along with another. Best friends, lovers, couples, siblings and even parents and their children have arguments. But that doesn't mean they give up on each other or insult each other. Don't you disagree with your parents? Does that mean you will give up on them? If not, then why should it be any different with your in-laws?' reasoned *masi*.

'But that's because they aren't my parents! And how do you know that they will treat me as they treat their son?'

'They will, if you be a daughter to them and treat them the way you treat your parents.'

'And how would I do that?'

'By leaving out your ego as far as they are concerned. Start with showing them proper respect. Respect will take you towards love for them. Once love exists, there is no place for anything else.'

'But how do I show them that respect?'

Masi replied, 'You must begin by following an important forgotten tradition daily.'

Think Tank

1. What was the important forgotten tradition that *masi* advised Shruti to follow?

2. What would following this tradition achieve?

The Think Tank encourages you to answer these questions on your own before referring to the answers given below.

Answers

1. The forgotten tradition *masi* mentioned was, to touch the feet of the elders and ask for their blessings daily after praying to God.

2. Bowing down before elder people and asking for their blessings is a sign of respect to them. Also, it is very difficult for both, the seeker of blessings and the one who gives the blessings, to bear ill feelings towards the other. Following this tradition daily would ensure that both harboured feelings of love towards each other.

74

'Why Do You Put Up With It?'

Samarjit was very forgetful. He was a renowned artist who lived in his own world. Most of the time, he was oblivious to his surroundings. His wife, Sayali put up with his forgetfulness patiently. She never complained. Of course, he loved her from the bottom of his heart, but he was always too occupied with some design, some work of art or some colour that had caught his fancy at that time.

On their fifth anniversary, Sayali baked him a lovely cake. Her sister too came to help her. But Samarjit had completely forgotten their anniversary. Even after he came home and saw the cake, he couldn't remember what it was for.

Sayali patiently reminded him and asked him to freshen up so that they could cut the cake. As he went along, her sister burst out, 'How do you put up with someone so absent-minded? I know he really loves you. But he is so irritating. He forgets all important days, leaves his shoes in the middle of the room and the rest of his things where he can't remember... and what not! Why don't you say something to him?'

———————————— **Think Tank** ————————————

1. What was Sayali's reply?

2. What is the moral of the story?

The Think Tank encourages you to answer these questions on your own before referring to the answers given below.

Answers

1. Sayali said, 'I don't say anything to him because affection is more important than perfection.'

2. We must remember that our love for our partner is more important than finding fault and complaining to him/her about how we have to suffer. Sayali knew that her husband loved her and this affection was more important to her than expecting any perfection from him.

75

Living On...

Roger was a positive thinker in and out. He always had a positive outlook on anything that happened. If his friend had a fracture, he would say, 'You should be grateful that you are alive. A fracture will heal soon.' Many times, his words ended up putting off people who didn't look at life from his point of view. If his wife complained that the maid wasn't coming for the next two days, he would say, 'Great! Don't cook. Let's go out for dinner on both days.' Though glad of the respite from cooking, his wife would warily wonder what solution he would have proposed, had the maid announced she would be taking the week off!

But nothing could dent Roger's positive attitude. Even when his young son aged 30 died after a long fight with cancer, he was only glad that his son's suffering was over and he was free at last. Now, at 62, he busied himself working with an orphanage, bringing joy and happiness into the lives of the many children who were deprived of life's basic necessities.

One day, when he was about to cross the road, he was aghast to find a young girl from the orphanage crossing the road, engrossed in talking to her doll. He also saw a few cars coming down the road at a speed that would surely crush the child. Without stopping to think, he rushed up to her and had just grabbed her in his arms when he was hit by a car. He held on to her so that she wouldn't be hurt when he fell on the road due to the impact.

They were taken to the hospital. The child was unhurt but the doctors declared his condition critical. It was impossible to save him, the doctors told his wife. Crying silently by his bedside, she asked him why he hadn't even thought about her and how she would live without him for the rest of her life. 'Look at the positive side, my dear. If you do, I shall be able to live on,' he said.

Think Tank

1. What was the positive side to this situation?

2. How would Roger live on?

The Think Tank encourages you to answer these questions on your own before referring to the answers given below.

Answers

1. The positive side of the situation was that Roger who had lived most of his life, had saved the young girl who would have either died or ended up being maimed for life.

2. Instead of mourning him, Roger wanted his wife to carry on his work of helping the children in the orphanage as his remembrance. He wanted her to understand that life was not only about living for oneself but also about being of help and offering a positive outlook to others. He would live on through her work.

76

Small Vs Big

Alice and her husband owned a bakery in a small town. They had taken a huge risk and put their little all into buying the bakery from an old friend who had retired. Alice put her heart and soul into baking and her husband managed the bakery.

Soon, word spread about Alice's baking and people of all ages thronged to their bakery for the most delicious cakes, pastries, buns, muffins and freshly baked bread. Encouraged by this response, the husband and wife duo strove to do even better. Instead of only offering standardized fare, they asked their customers what they would regularly like to buy and worked hard to develop the right flavour for each item they produced. Thus, they knew exactly what each family liked to have, and the special occasions on which they required it too. Alice's husband maintained an entire database of the special days, like birthdays or wedding anniversaries of their customers and their families.

Soon, they had to appoint two assistants for baking. But Alice did not leave the baking to them. She ensured that each of her customers got exactly what they wanted. She also did research on recipes and ingredients with a view to offering something new. Many women brought her their age-old family recipes, some of which she included in her usual items. Similarly, her husband had to appoint two people at the counter, but he too never left the sales entirely to them. He always attended to all his customers himself. The entire town – young and old alike, was in love with the bakery and its owners.

However, one day a multinational food company, which wanted to make inroads into the small town, contacted them and persuaded them to sell their business for a huge sum. Despite much pressure and persuasion, they refused.

Finally, the company opened its shop at another place quite close to Alice's bakery. It had double the frontage, lovely lighting and an artistic decor. There were about 5-6 trained attendants and an equal number of trained bakers. It organized a fancy opening ceremony, calling a well-known film star for its inauguration. The company was expecting huge profits from this bakery.

The festival season was not too bad, but later, the new bakery didn't do too well, while Alice's bakery was still running successfully. The management of the company were shocked to note that in spite of all their investment – the best bakers, superb decor and professionally-trained staff, their bakery was not doing well. One of the managers came down to check why this was happening. He was aghast to know the reasons.

Think Tank

1. Why was the new bakery not doing as well as Alice's Bakery?

2. What is the lesson to be learnt from this story?

The Think Tank encourages you to answer these questions on your own before referring to the answers given below.

Answers

1. The new bakery had been set up by the company only to make profits. Despite the fantastic decor, polite staff and expert bakers, it lacked the personal touch and comfort that Alice's small bakery provided people. While Alice knew exactly what each of her customers liked, and lovingly baked for them, the new bakery only sold profitable, standardized products without understanding what people wanted. The staff was polite and helpful but there was no personal attention or comfort in their conversation with the people. Thus, people were not attracted to the new bakery.

2. A business succeeds due to the love of its customers. No matter how huge a business, if it is not in touch with what customers want, it will not become successful.

77

Get Out of Yourself

'I am still not feeling well,' said Suhas for the umpteenth time. 'What's the use in telling you? I'll have to go to office just the same,' he continued. Shalini sighed. True, he had been ill for some time, but the doctor had given him a clean bill of health just yesterday. How could he still feel unwell? she wondered.

She reflected on their lives. They had everything they could possibly want, and yet, Suhas was never really happy. It had been bearable till his mother had been alive. But ever since her death one year ago, he had begun to fall ill very often. He had had the best of treatments and care, but it looked like nothing could cure him. Him or his attitude? thought Shalini. Others in the family, like his aged father, Shalini and the children too missed his mother. But they had come to terms with it.

Suhas had always been the complaining kind. Nothing was too good or great according to him. Though he wasn't mean, he was quite self-centred. Many a times, he couldn't see beyond himself.

Shalini decided to do something about it. She took him to see a doctor who lived quite far off. 'Is he a specialist?' asked the sceptical Suhas.

'No. He is Sheena's family doctor and he's very good,' said Shalini.

The doctor patiently heard his health problems and went over his earlier reports. He scribbled a few words on a prescription, put it in an envelope and told him to open it after going home, but only when he was alone.

'When should I come to see you again?' asked Suhas. 'You won't have to, if you follow the prescription,' said the doctor.

'But what if I don't understand the prescription, Doctor?'

'Well, you must reflect on it till you do.'

Suhas eagerly went home, locked himself in his room and opened the prescription. To his intense surprise and dismay, it contained only four words -

'GET OUT OF YOURSELF'

A week later Shalini called the doctor to thank him.

Think Tank

1. What did the doctor mean by the prescription?

2. What is the lesson to be learnt from the story?

The Think Tank encourages you to answer these questions on your own before referring to the answers given below.

Answers

1. Through the prescription, the doctor had made Suhas aware of his obsession with his own sorrow and the effect it was having

on his health. He hadn't realized that his mother's death had also been a loss to others in his family like his aged father, his wife or his children. If Suhas was so badly affected, imagine how much his father must have been suffering. Instead of being a pillar of strength for his family, he was acting as though he was the only one who was suffering. Through the prescription, the doctor was telling him to look beyond his own needs.

2. When tragedy befalls, your loved ones are also affected. They might be younger, weaker or more vulnerable than you. At such times, it is your duty to be strong and help them get over their sorrow.

78

The Secret Affair

Susan was sure her husband was having an affair. There were small indications – he had begun to spend time away from her; usually keen to accompany her everywhere, nowadays he had started avoiding it; earlier, whenever she went out anywhere, he would always ask her what time she would be back, but nowadays he didn't...

Moreover, he had also begun to lie. When she had recently stayed at a cousin's place, he hadn't mentioned going away on his own for a holiday. But when she came back, the maid told her that there had been no one at home for three days.

It was really unlike him. A well-educated banker with a good reputation, Arnold was essentially a family man. He loved the children and Susan and made sure he provided his family with everything they required.

Susan thought she had begun to notice the change in him after her mother's death some time ago. What was wrong? she wondered. Was it her? She was sure there was nothing on the face of it. She was popular among his friends, cousins and family and had easily adapted herself to them. The exception was his mother. Susan somehow hadn't been able to get along with her mother-in-law.

But her mother-in-law had been living separately in the same city for many years now.

She decided she had to know. One evening when the children were away, she confronted him.

'Are you seeing someone?' she asked him outright.

Taking a deep breath and looking her straight in the eye, he said, 'Yes.'

'I feared as much,' she said quietly. 'Since when?'

'After your mother's death,' he said.

'How could you even say this to me?' she asked.

'It's the truth,' he said quietly.

Suddenly she looked at him shocked. 'Do you mean it's Anne?'

Anne was her younger sister.

'Good Lord, Susan! Anne's always been a kid to me.'

'Then who is it? Someone I know?'

'Yes.'

'How could you even think of getting involved with someone I know?' she shrieked.

'I loved her even before you came into my life and I shall always love her till I die.'

'I want to know who she is...'

'Sure,' he said. He strode to the mantelpiece and picked up one of the photo frames and gave it to her.

Teary-eyed, Susan looked into the face of her mother-in-law.

Think Tank

1. Why was Arnold meeting his mother secretly?

2. What was the lesson that Susan learnt?

3. What is the moral of this story?

The Think Tank encourages you to answer these questions on your own before referring to the answers given below.

Answers

1. Arnold had drifted away from his mother because Susan didn't get along with her. Due to his family commitments he was rarely able to meet her. But after Susan lost her mother, he realized that his mother was getting old too. He realized her place in his life and that she too needed his love and so he began to spend time with her. He did so secretly because he didn't want Susan to be hurt about it.

2. Susan realized that while all these years she had always been there for her mother, Arnold had not been able to spend much time with his mother. She lived elsewhere and did not visit them as Susan and she didn't get along. He had lost out on precious time that he could have spent with his mother.

She also needed to reflect on the fact that her husband had not been able to share his concerns about his mother with her due to her troubled relationship with her mother-in-law.

3. Each relationship that we have is special and should be treated that way. People do not last forever. They leave when their time comes. It is up to us to make time for the relationships that are special to us.

79

A Fly in the Tea

Yogesh's father always felt that his child's generation had moved too far away from Nature and that was the cause of all their ills. Addicted to TV's, mobiles, PC's and tabs, they had no compassion for Nature. The plants and animals they knew were the ones that they had seen only in their textbooks. So when he came across an organization that conducted treks for teenage children, he immediately enrolled Yogesh and asked his friends to enroll their children too. 'Your son will come back a very different person altogether,' the guide assured Yogesh's father.

On the first day, the trek began very early in the morning. By around 10am, most of the children were exhausted and the guide stopped at a little inn for them to refresh themselves with some tea.

As the children were having their tea, Yogesh got up and screamed, 'Good God! There's a fly in my tea!' The guide immediately got up and told him to calm down. He instructed the owner to give Yogesh another glass of tea. Meanwhile, the guide carefully picked up the fly and went out.

After some time, Yogesh was given another glass of tea. After he finished drinking it, the young helper in the inn came running to the guide with a happy smile and said...

Yogesh was ashamed of his behaviour.

Think Tank

1. What did the young helper say to the guide?

2. What is the implication of this story?

The Think Tank encourages you to answer these questions on your own before referring to the answers given below.

Answers

1. The helper came up to the guide and said, '*Sirji*, thank you for your help. The fly will live.'

2. We feel that insects like the fly are an interruption in our world. However, it is also true that we are an interruption in their world. Just like we have a right to live, so do other living beings. This is what the guide demonstrated to the children.

80

Let Me Die Instead of Him!

Nirmala's grandson fell ill very often. His parents were worried sick. They consulted many doctors, but none of them could diagnose the exact problem.

Nirmala, worried about her grandson's future would often say, 'O God! Why do you trouble this poor child? Let him be alive and well. I am old and have lived my life. Take me if you must!' She also repeated the same thing to everyone she met.

One day, God decided to test her and appeared to her in a dream and said, 'I have come for you. It is time for you to die!'

Suddenly, Nirmala woke up screaming and said...

---------------------- **Think Tank** ----------------------

1. What did Nirmala say?

2. What is the implication of this story?

The Think Tank encourages you to answer these questions on your own before referring to the answers given below.

Answers

1. Nirmala said, 'Spare me, Lord! I am hale and hearty. My grandson is sick all the time. Take him if you must!'

2. It is easy to say that we want to die in place of someone else. But when the time comes to actually face death, we cling to life even more desperately. Nirmala understood this when she was actually faced with the prospect of death.

81

Mother Will Understand

Rocky had it all. A fantastic job as a photographer, the opportunity to learn and travel all over the world… The only problem was that he had to leave his mother alone at home in Mumbai. He would be away for weeks at a stretch and would hardly get to see his mother even on weekends when he was in Mumbai. But that's just the way things were, he thought. His mother too understood the pressures of his job and encouraged him.

Once, he had gone to Canada for an assignment. It was his mother's birthday in the next week and Rocky had planned to get back to be with her. But the company was offering him a training course for which he had to stay back in Canada. That meant he couldn't be with his mother on her birthday. But he was sure she would understand; she always did!

One day, as he was walking along the street, he came across a flower shop with the most beautiful flowers he had ever seen. *Mother would love them*, he thought. He asked the florist to pack them and have them delivered to his address in Mumbai. It was the least he could do.

As he walked out, he noticed a little boy look longingly at the flowers. He bent to ask the boy what was wrong. The boy told him that he wanted flowers for his mother but had no money. 'That's no problem. I'll buy you whatever you want,' said Rocky and bought the flowers the boy wanted.

'Sir, could you also drop me? I have no money for the fare either.' Rocky could only reply in the affirmative. He went with the boy to his destination. Surprisingly, the boy took him to a graveyard. 'Here is my mother,' he said, pointing to a grave.

Think Tank

1. What was Rocky's reaction to the boy's words?

2. What is the moral of this story?

The Think Tank encourages you to answer these questions on your own before referring to the answers given below.

Answers

1. Rocky was stunned. He cancelled his training and went home to be with his mother on her birthday.

2. We conveniently assume that our loved ones will understand the situation we are in and adjust accordingly. We take it for granted that they will always be with us all our lives. However, if we do not value their time and their needs, one day, without our realizing it, they may go away from our lives forever. It is important for us to value their presence in our lives while they are still with us.

82

The Compulsory Marriage

Once upon a time, there was a rich merchant called Dhyanchand. He had two daughters – Rohini and Rupa. Rupa was the younger one and was cheerful and beautiful. Rohini, the elder one was very dutiful but she wasn't as pretty as Rupa. However, Rohini was her father's favourite due to her calm and understanding nature. The merchant was looking for suitable grooms for them both.

This was the time when a man was allowed to have more than one wives. It was expected that he should treat all his wives in a just and fair manner.

Rajat, the handsome son of a landlord had been in love with Rupa for some time. He went to Dhyanchand to ask for Rupa's hand in marriage. Dhyanchand however wanted Rohini to be married first as she was the elder one. Also, he felt that Rajat was a more suitable match for her.

But seeing that Rajat wanted to marry Rupa, Dhyanchand stated his condition that Rajat could marry Rupa provided he also married Rohini. Rajat tried to convince Dhyanchand that he was not interested in Rohini, but Dhyanchand was adamant.

Seeing that there was no choice, Rajat agreed to marry Rohini too. After the marriage, Rajat completely devoted himself to Rupa. He paid no attention to Rohini and she had to live on her own. Though she too loved Rajat, he did not love her. Rajat and Rupa were inseparable. Rohini felt like an outsider among their midst. Rupa too, did nothing to help her sister.

After a year of living this way, Rohini complained to her father about Rajat's behaviour. She told him that she didn't want to stay with Rajat anymore. When Dhyanchand questioned Rajat, he too said that he didn't love Rohini and didn't want to stay with her. Dhyanchand was furious! Rajat was trying to get out of the very commitment he had given Dhyanchand. Dhyanchand decided to take the matter to the king. The king was a wise and just man. He heard each one's story.

Dhyanchand told him that Rajat had already agreed to his condition to marry Rohini, so he must give her the love and respect that he gave Rupa.

Rajat said that he had never wanted to marry Rohini but Dhyanchand had given him no choice. He had no ill feelings towards Rohini, but what could he do if he didn't love her?

Rohini told the king that initially she had agreed to the marriage only because of her love for her father. After marriage, she had fallen in love with Rajat and couldn't stand being neglected by him. That is why she wanted to return to her father's house.

Think Tank

1. Who was the victim in this case and who was guilty?

2. What was the king's verdict?

The Think Tank encourages you to answer these questions on your own before referring to the answers given below.

Answers

1. Rohini was the victim because she knew that Rajat didn't want to marry her but she still agreed because she wanted to obey her father's wish. She also gave Rajat the love and respect that a wife should give her husband, but was neglected by him. Rajat was guilty because he had married Rohini knowing that he did not love her and had no intention of treating her fairly.

2. The king's verdict was that Rajat should accept Rohini as his wife and give her the love and respect she deserved. She had done no wrong and had been dutiful in her conduct. She was Rajat's responsibility as Rajat had married her. The king also felt that asking Rohini to stay at her father's house would defeat the very purpose of the institution of marriage and set a very wrong example for others.

83

Understanding Anger

Lord Buddha once asked his disciples – 'Why is it that two people speak loudly and aggressively when they are angry with each other, even if they are sitting close to one another?'

All the disciples thought about it but they couldn't come up with an answer.

Lord Buddha then asked them another question – 'Why is it that when two people are in love, even eye contact or body language is enough to communicate their feelings to each other, even if they are standing far off from each other?'

Again none of the disciples could answer the question. They asked Lord Buddha for the answer.

─────────── **Think Tank** ───────────

1. What was the answer that Lord Buddha gave them?

_____

The Think Tank encourages you to answer the question on your own before referring to the answer given below.

Answer

1. When two people are angry with each other, the distance between their hearts increases. Their minds are far away from each other. That is why, even if they are physically close to each other, they speak loudly and aggressively. But when two people are in love, their hearts and minds are close to each other. So they don't have to speak loudly even if they are far away from each other. Even a gesture is enough for them to communicate.

84

Not My Dog

Shreya was very lonely. Back from her boarding school for the holidays, she was mostly alone the entire day. Her parents were at work and till they got back there was no one to play with her. She had no friends because she knew nobody around. Sometimes her maid's daughter would come to spend time with her, if she was free.

On Shreya's birthday, her uncle gave her a puppy. Her happiness knew no bounds. A puppy changed things entirely.

She named it Snowy because it was white all over and tied a red ribbon round its neck. She spent a happy week playing with it. Her maid's daughter too came to play with it.

But one morning, the puppy just disappeared. Shreya and the maid's daughter looked high and low for it, but it was nowhere to be found. Shreya was sad and depressed. Nothing anybody said could bring her out of her sorrow.

One day, her maid's daughter came running to tell her that she had seen Snowy with a boy of about ten years. She had followed the boy and knew where he lived. Shreya immediately went with her to meet the boy.

They went through very narrow roads into the slum area of town. They came to a building which was being constructed. 'First floor,' said the maid's daughter. They ran up to the first floor. There, Shreya saw a woman cooking food on a *chulha*. A boy of around ten years was sitting near her with a book in his hand. In front of him, was a young boy of around four. And there in his lap was Snowy.

Snowy was playing with the boy. He ran out of the boy's lap but instead of following him, the boy sat and patiently waited till Snowy came back to him. The boy was paralyzed waist-down.

The maid's daughter went up to the woman and told her that it was their dog. The elder boy looked at the mother quietly. 'Where did you find him, Raju?' the mother asked. 'I found him on the streets. I thought he would be a good companion to Chotu,' he answered.

The maid's daughter once more pointed out that it was their dog. 'Are you sure it is yours?' asked the boy. The maid's daughter nodded confidently adding that they had tied the red ribbon around his neck. The boy reluctantly scooped Snowy in his arms and began to bring him to the girls. The small boy immediately let out a wail and tried to get up from his place to prevent his brother from giving the dog. But he couldn't move.

The boy gave the dog to Shreya. The small boy was still crying loudly. Shreya looked at the dog carefully and gave it back to the boy.

'Sorry,' she said. 'It's not ours,' and turned to leave.

Think Tank
---

1. Why did Shreya give back the dog knowing that it was hers?

The Think Tank encourages you to answer the question on your own before referring to the answer given below.

Answer

1. Shreya saw that the young boy who couldn't walk was playing with the dog. Like her, there was no one who could play with him and additionally, he too couldn't go anywhere. The puppy was his sole companion. So she sacrificed the puppy so that the young boy could be with him. His happiness was more important than her loneliness.

85

Strong Medicine

Raina and Rohit were a middle aged couple. While Raina was an optimist and always looked at the bright side of things, Rohit was hot-tempered, found fault with most things and was very doubtful about everything he came across. He rarely trusted people and his subordinates also complained that he always found fault with their work. Nothing could easily satisfy him, nor would he praise something that he found good.

Once, they had gone for a family picnic to a friend's farmhouse. It was the rainy season and both of them developed stomach infections. Since they were both unwell and couldn't wait to get to their family doctor, they went to a doctor who was nearby.

Rohit though unwell, was a little uneasy about this. The doctor didn't have a posh clinic like their family doctor, but judging from the line of patients outside, he was quite popular. He gave them both medicines and asked them to come back after a week. 'Are you sure I will feel better in a week?' asked Rohit. 'Of course, you will,' replied the doctor.

When they left the doctor's place, Rohit told Raina, 'I'm not too sure of the quality of medicines given by this doctor chap. I hope they work.' Throughout the journey home he went on about how this doctor didn't seem to be as well-qualified as their family doctor and how he wasn't quite confident about his treatment.

Both of them took their doses daily. Raina began to recover in the next three days. But Rohit didn't recover. His stomach pain was as bad as ever. 'I knew his medicines wouldn't work,' said Rohit. Raina told him they would go to the doctor and ask him what was wrong.

When they went back to the doctor, Rohit said triumphantly, 'I was sure these medicines wouldn't work, Doctor.' Raina, in an embarrassed voice asked the doctor how come she had recovered while Rohit hadn't.

Think Tank

1. What did the doctor say?

2. What is the moral of this story?

The Think Tank encourages you to answer these questions on your own before referring to the answers given below.

Answers

1. The doctor said, 'I made a mistake. While preparing the medicine, I added a large dose of faith to your wife's medicine, while I completely forgot to add faith to your dose. That's why she got better and you didn't.'

2. Apart from a doctor's medicines, faith plays a large role in our healing. If we have our medicines believing that we will never get better, no matter how strong the medicine is, it will have no effect. All things are possible if we just have a little faith.

86

Krishna's Flute

The *Gopis* of Vrindavan were jealous of Krishna's flute. While each one of them longed for his company, it was only his flute which was always with him. He carried it everywhere he went.

Once, they decided to ask the flute what her secret was. Why was only she given the honour of being with him while they had to wait to even catch a glimpse of him? Did she know any magic? Was there a special scent she had? Was she made out of some special material?

The flute answered that neither was she made of any special material, nor did she have any special scent. She knew no magic either. She further told them that she didn't even play her own music.

This surprised the *Gopis*. They asked her, 'How is it possible that you can be with Krishna if you don't even play your own music? And what about the music that we hear from you?' To which the flute replied...

Think Tank

1. What did the flute reply?

The Think Tank encourages you to answer the question on your own before referring to the answer given below.

Answer

1. The flute replied that she had submitted entirely to Krishna. She played no music of her own. She played only the music that Krishna wanted to play. That is why she could always be with him.

87

Prove Your Faith

That year, the rains were late. The village wells were fast drying up and the heat was unbearable. Panditji was the last resort. The villagers flocked to him for advice.

He said, 'I was already pondering over the problem. I had a dream yesterday. The Rain God told me that He was testing our faith. He said, 'You villagers should prove your faith in me. Only then will you get rain.'

The villagers gaped. Panditji continued, 'I advise that we organize a *yagna* (fire sacrifice), to prove our faith in the Rain God and appease Him.' The villagers agreed.

Soon, the entire village was caught up in frenzied activity, preparing for the *yagna* which would prove their faith to the Rain God. The village headman himself oversaw each arrangement.

The day of the *yagna* dawned bright and sunny. Everyone was dressed in their best and prepared to ensure that everything went well. They were eager to assure the Rain God of their faith in Him. The *yagna* began. Each offering was made with positivity and hope and each mantra was uttered with devotion. All the villagers gathered together, sat with their hands folded in prayer.

As the time drew closer for the *yagna* to end, the villagers began to get restless. There was no sign of rain… not even clouds. Everyone began to look at Panditji questioningly, as he went on with the *yagna*. They then spoke to the village headman. 'What is wrong? Is there something missing? Haven't we proved our faith? Have we forgotten anything?' they asked him.

The headman looked at his list to check if they had missed out on any of the requirements. But they hadn't. Just then, the headman's young son cried, '*Babuji*, we have forgotten the most important thing to show our faith. But don't worry, we will get it.' He got up, gathered all his friends and they all ran towards their houses.

Soon, a small army of children came carrying what would assure the Rain God of the faith of the villagers.

―――――――――   **Think Tank**   ―――――――――

1. What was it that the young boys brought to show their faith to the Rain God?

The Think Tank encourages you to answer the question on your own before referring to the answer given below.

Answer

1. The boys had brought umbrellas.

88

The Haunted House

The Haunted House was a favourite topic among Ratan and his friends. Situated about two kilometres from his house, it had stood there for as long as he and even his father remembered. Strange stories had been spread about it and it was a topic of discussion for many an evening among youngsters and elders alike. Of course, Ratan's mother had warned him never to go near the house. She had even advised him to take another longer route to his school so that he wouldn't pass the haunted house on the way.

One day he had gone to his friend's house to play. As he left, his friend's mother asked him to drop her maidservant's son, a young boy of about nine years, on his way home. Ratan and the young boy started off. Ratan asked him where he lived. The boy pointed out the road to his home.

Ratan felt a tiny chill creep up his spine. That was the road which went up to the haunted house. This meant that he would have to go past the haunted house. He thought of refusing but he had to drop the boy home.

As they passed along the haunted house, Ratan said every prayer he knew. Finally, the boy turned at the end of the wall of the haunted house. There, he pointed out to his house. It was a shanty which was built right next to the haunted house. 'You live here!' exclaimed Ratan. The boy nodded. Just then, the boy's elder sister came from the gate of the haunted house, carrying two pots of water.

'How can you live next to this house? How can your sister fill water from that house? Don't you know that it is haunted?' Ratan asked the boy.

Think Tank

1. What was the boy's answer?

2. What is the implication of this story?

The Think Tank encourages you to answer these questions on your own before referring to the answers given below.

Answers

1. The boy said, 'Maybe it is haunted. Some people say so. But we have never seen any ghosts there. We only know that this is the only place we can call home and the tap inside the gate of the house is our only source of water.'

2. We easily believe in ghosts and avoid haunted houses because we can afford to believe in them and avoid them. But ghosts and haunted houses have no importance for those fighting for basic necessities and survival.

89

A Matter of Outlook

Sridhar had a habit of discussing his experiences with his mentor. Generally, his mentor never argued with him or told him that he was wrong. He would only show him an example that proved what he wanted to say.

Once, Sridhar told his mentor that he had experienced that a person's character, behaviour, nature and personality was dependent on his environment and the experiences he had in his young years.

The mentor smiled and said, 'Let's check this theory of yours.' He took him to the house of his late driver. The driver's wife and his elder son welcomed them. The elder son was working in the mentor's company.

About half an hour later, the younger son came in. He was in a drunken state and had to be led into the other room by his elder brother, who closed the door after him. The room now smelled of liquor.

The elder son apologized for his brother's behaviour. From the conversation, Sridhar gathered that the boy's father, i.e., his mentor's late driver had died of alcohol addiction when the boys were teenagers. After some time, his mentor took their leave. He then asked Sridhar, 'What have you learnt from this story?'

--------------------------- **Think Tank** ---------------------------

1. What was Sridhar's answer?

_____

The Think Tank encourages you to answer the question on your own before referring to the answer given below.

Answer

1. Though a person's character does get shaped by his environment and his experiences, his own attitude/outlook towards his experiences is also very important. In the case of the driver's sons, while the elder one saw his father's plight and decided that he would never touch alcohol, but would be independent and support his family, the younger son went completely under his father's influence and began drinking at a young age.

90

The Spilt Bowl of Sambar

Each time Isha went to her parents' place she found she learnt another lesson in parenting. This time, the occasion was her parents' wedding anniversary celebration in their new house.

Her parents had just built a new bungalow. They had used all their imagination and put in each and every small thing that they had wanted in their house but hadn't been able to afford for so long. They had also got it decorated by an interior decorator who had put in wonderful fittings, lovely paintings and a wonderful carpet to match.

Isha knew the ruckus her daughter, Sonia could create and she had already warned her that she was to ensure that she did nothing to spoil anything in *nana's* new house.

Isha's mother had made *idli sambar* for the little ones and Sonia was carrying hers in a bowl filled up to the brim when she tripped over a table sending the bowl flying out of her little hands. The *sambar* was spilled all over the new carpet.

Sonia got up and saw the mess she had created. Crying, she ran into the kitchen where *nani* and Isha were filling bowls with *sambar*. '*Nani*, I'm so sorry. I've spilt my bowl of *sambar* all over the carpet in the hall,' she said sobbing. Isha looked shocked.

Nani smiled at Sonia, knelt down to her and said…

Think Tank

1. What did *nani* say to Sonia?

2. What is the implication of this story?

The Think Tank encourages you to answer these questions on your own before referring to the answers given below.

Answers

1. *Nani* said, 'It's okay Sonia, I have made plenty of *sambar*. You can have as much as you want.'

2. Children will be children. Though it is necessary to discipline them, it is also essential for grown-ups to realize that they will take their own time to understand. If they realize their mistakes, it is better to forgive them and forget the issue.

91

Hard Work Pays

Ravi was a star salesman of his company which published various magazines. Month after month he achieved his targets and became an icon for his colleagues. Even sales people handling other magazines were sent to him for field training. The sales person would accompany Ravi who began his sales calls early in the morning.

Everybody who accompanied him on sales calls including his bosses were aghast at the number of calls that he made in a day. Whether a call was successful or whether the would-be client banged the door in his face, Ravi simply went on to the next call with equal gusto.

It was mind-blowing. Everyone wondered how he did it. At the company's annual function, Ravi's name was announced for the Employee of the Year Award. As he collected his award, the Managing Director (MD), who had heard quite a lot about him asked him to address the audience. After the expression of gratitude, Ravi began to leave the stage when the MD stopped him. He said that there was something everybody present wanted to know — how could Ravi go from one sales call to the next with equal enthusiasm, irrespective of the outcome of his first call?

Think Tank

1. What was Ravi's answer?

The Think Tank encourages you to answer the question on your own before referring to the answer given below.

Answer

1. Ravi said, 'It's simple, Sir. If the first call of the day is good, I tell myself, 'It's my lucky day. I must work hard today.' If the first call of the day doesn't work out, I tell myself, 'Today looks a little difficult. I must work hard today.'

92

One Half-Ticket

Amarnath had taken his twelve-year-old son to the amusement park. He knew the tickets were expensive, but after all, he thought, the fun in visiting the park was when the boy was still young enough to enjoy it.

The ticket counter was deserted except for the man at the counter. Amarnath asked the man for two tickets for adults. The man asked him how old his son was. Amarnath replied that he was 12.

The man said, 'Sir, if you want, I can give you one ticket for an adult and one for a child. Children up to 11 years can go on half-ticket. No one would know the difference.'

---------- **Think Tank** ----------

1. What did Amarnath reply?

2. What is the implication of this story?

The Think Tank encourages you to answer these questions on your own before referring to the answers given below.

Answers

1. Amarnath said, 'My son would know the difference.'

2. Children emulate the behaviour of their parents. Therefore, parents need to be careful how they behave. Had Amarnath accepted the man's advice, it would have created the wrong impression on his son's mind forever.

93

Karna,
the Unparalleled Donor

Karna, the great Mahabharata warrior was also known as *Daanveer* Karna – the great donor. Once, Arjuna asked Krishna, 'What is it about Karna that makes him such a great and ideal donor? Why am I not known to be equal to him in this respect?'

Krishna smiled and decided to teach Arjuna why. They were passing by some mountains. With a snap of his fingers Krishna turned the mountains to gold. Then he said, 'Arjuna, you must give away these mountains of gold to the people of this village. Only, ensure that every bit of the gold is given away.'

Happily, Arjuna called the villagers, announcing that he would be donating gold. This made them very happy and they followed him to the mountains of gold singing his praises. Arjuna proudly took his place and began to give away gold to each of the villagers. This went on for two days. However, the gold simply did not reduce. Arjuna was tired. He told Krishna that he wanted to rest, as it was now impossible for him to donate any more gold.

Then Krishna called Karna and told him to donate the mountains of gold and ensure that all the gold was distributed.

---------------- **Think Tank** ----------------

1. How did Karna distribute the mountains of gold?

2. What is the moral of this story?

The Think Tank encourages you to answer these questions on your own before referring to the answers given below.

Answers

1. Karna simply called out to the villagers and told them to take the mountains of gold and left.

2. Even though Arjuna gave away the gold, he was actually fascinated by it. So he involved himself in giving it away to the villagers. He gave each villager the amount that he thought was right. He was also happy with the villagers' praise of him. On the other hand, Karna just gave away the mountains of gold without expecting any praise or blessings from the people. Thus, he proved himself an unparalleled donor.

94

Karna – The Great Donor

There is another story of Karna, the great donor.

When Karna was a young boy, a Brahmin came to his door. He asked Karna to give him a handful of grain as alms.

Karna went into the house and brought a bag full of grains and gave it to the Brahmin. The Brahmin said, 'Young boy, I had asked you only for a handful of grains. Why have you given me so much?'

The Brahmin was amazed at Karna's answer.

--------- **Think Tank** ---------

1. What was Karna's answer?

2. What is the moral of this story?

The Think Tank encourages you to answer these questions on your own before referring to the answers given below.

Answers

1. Karna replied, 'O Holy One, my hand is quite small. Had I given you a handful of grains, it would have been an injustice to you.'

2. Karna was indeed a great donor. Not only was he able to give away things without expectation, but he was also able to think from the receiver's point of view.

95

Patience

A group of people had come together to understand spirituality. Swamiji was addressing the group. The topic for that day was 'patience'. One man stood up and asked, 'Swamiji, what is 'patience'?'

Everyone was eager to understand what patience was. But Swamiji said, 'Friends, I have forgotten what patience is. Will you wait for five minutes and let me gather my thoughts on it?' The audience was disappointed, but they nodded in agreement.

After five minutes, Swamiji got up to answer the question.

Think Tank

1. What was Swamiji's answer?

The Think Tank encourages you to answer the question on your own before referring to the answer given below.

Answer

1. Swamiji said, 'All of you were eager to hear my answer. But even then you waited for five minutes. That, friends, is 'patience'.'

96

The Readiness to Improve

Somnath was an executive with a publishing firm. Ravi was an office assistant who sometimes helped him during dispatches to retailers. While Somnath was an MBA, Ravi had come up the hard way, starting work as a peon. Later, he had studied, learnt computers and begun to work as an office assistant.

During the dispatch for an important order, Somnath and Ravi ended up sending the wrong books. When the retailer complained, their boss came to know about it. Their boss was known to be a fair man. He called both of them and pointed out the mistake. On knowing about the mistake, Somnath argued that he had been given very little time to organize the order. He went on to say that he had also been involved in organizing other dispatches and had been really busy. He also said that at least Ravi should have looked into the order and brought the mistake to his notice.

Their boss then asked Ravi what his explanation for the mistake was. Ravi simply said, 'I am sorry, Sir. I will be more careful in the future.'

Their boss issued a memo to Somnath, but didn't issue one to Ravi. Somnath was incensed at this. He asked his boss the reason for his partiality. If both had committed the same mistake, why was only he being punished for it?

His boss said...

Think Tank
---

1. What did his boss say?

The Think Tank encourages you to answer the question on your own before referring to the answer given below.

Answer

1. His boss said, 'People are punished so that they improve on their mistakes. While Ravi has learnt a lesson and is ready to improve himself, you aren't even ready to accept your mistake. Therefore, the memo.'

97

To Tell You the Truth

Bansilal used to go to a sweetmeat shop daily. He had a standard order of one glass of rose milk. This went on for some years.

One day, just after Bansilal had drunk milk and left, the owner of the shop discovered that there was a huge dead cockroach in the vessel in which the milk was stored. He was extremely worried that he had served contaminated milk to his clients. He was especially worried about Bansilal, who came to his shop daily. He hoped to God that he hadn't fallen ill.

He waited to see Bansilal the next day. But Bansilal didn't come that day, nor the next, nor the next. By now, the owner was extremely worried. He wondered if Bansilal was suffering from food poisoning or much worse, if he had succumbed to it!

No! Please God! Don't let that happen!, he prayed.

However, the next day allayed all his fears. In walked Bansilal as radiant as ever and ordered his glass of rose milk. The owner's relief knew no bounds! He went up to Bansilal and asked him, 'Where had you been, Sir? Why didn't you come to my shop for the last week?'

The surprised Bansilal mentioned that he had been out of town. The owner was relieved. Bansilal asked him the reason behind his question. The owner told him, 'To tell you the truth, when you came to my shop a few days ago, you were served milk from the container which had a dead cockroach. I was worried whether this had affected your health and you had developed food poisoning due to it. When you didn't come for so many days, I was further worried that maybe you had succumbed to food poisoning.' A startled Bansilal got up and left the shop.

Two days later, the owner came to know that Bansilal had died due to food poisoning.

Think Tank

1. Why did Bansilal die after hearing the story?

2. What is the moral of this story?

The Think Tank encourages you to answer these questions on your own before referring to the answers given below.

Answers

1. What people don't know can't hurt them. The same was the case with Bansilal. As long as he believed there was nothing wrong with the milk, he was even able to digest the contaminated milk. But when he came to know about it, he lost his capacity to digest even the good milk and due to the knowledge that he had drunk contaminated milk, he suffered from food poisoning and died.

2. Don't tell people truths which are pointless. You gain nothing by doing so and disturb the person unnecessarily.

98

Setting an Example

Meghnad came home from work much later than usual. His wife too had had a bad day at work. As he sat down for dinner with his ten-year-old son, his wife quickly served them.

Suddenly his son shrieked, 'Mom! This curry tastes so awful.' Meghnad's wife looked as though she had been struck and said, 'I am so sorry dear, what's wrong with it?'

Her son continued, 'It's just plain awful. I can't eat it.'

Meghnad quietly looked at his son and said, 'There is no need to shout. I'm eating the curry too. If you feel it lacks something, you can add salt or spices to it, to suit your taste.' His son finished the curry silently.

Later, when his wife had her dinner, she realized that the curry contained no spices and no salt either. She asked her husband why he had said nothing when their son told her that the curry tasted awful.

───────────── **Think Tank** ─────────────

1. What was Meghnad's reply?

2. What is the implication of this story?

The Think Tank encourages you to answer these questions on your own before referring to the answers given below.

Answers

1. Meghnad said, 'When our son grows up, he won't remember the taste of the curry, but he will certainly remember my words and my actions. I had to set an example.'

2. Children learn expected behaviour from their parents. Had Meghnad reacted like his son had, not only would it have hurt his wife, but his son would have thought that such behaviour was acceptable. Meghnad wanted to ensure that his son did not pick up this habit and so, he controlled his own behaviour first.

99

A Teacher's Responsibility

Acharya Shripad had many pupils who lived with him in his ashram. But there was a boy among them who was a thief. *Acharya* Shripad knew about it but said nothing to the boy. One day, a few other boys caught the boy red-handed. They brought him to the *Acharya* but he said nothing to the boy. The rest of them didn't understand their teacher's conduct, but they kept quiet.

A few days later, again the same boy was caught stealing by the others. Once again, their teacher said and did nothing. Now this angered the students and they decided to ask their teacher to send the boy back home. None of them wanted to study with a boy who was a thief. 'But what if *Acharya* yet again says or does nothing? What shall we do then?' asked one of them.

The eldest among them replied, 'Then there remains only one thing to be done. *Acharya* will have to make a choice – whether this boy stays, or we do.'

They went to the *Acharya* and asked him to dismiss the boy else, they would all leave. The *Acharya* said, 'I would be truly sorry to lose you all and yet, I cannot ask that boy to leave.'

This angered the students. They asked him, 'How can you be ready to lose us, but not him?'

The *Acharya's* answer brought the thief and the other boys to their senses.

Think Tank

1. What was the *Acharya's* answer?

The Think Tank encourages you to answer the question on your own before referring to the answer given below.

Answer

1. The *Acharya* said, 'I am ready to let you all go because any teacher would be proud to teach you. But what about this boy? No other teacher will be willing to teach him due to his habits. So it is my responsibility to teach him. I cannot ask him to leave.'

100

God Bless You!

Satyavan had to go to the Shiva temple on Mondays. His mother had told him to. She had also told him that he should offer milk to Lord Shiva.

The temple was always crowded and he had to leave early from office to reach in time for the *aarti*.

That day, there was a huge line of people waiting to buy milk and an even bigger line for the *darshan*. While he waited impatiently for the *darshan*, a beggar was walking down the line of the waiting people, asking for food. Most people ignored the beggar and shooed him away. When he came up to Satyavan, Satyavan shouted at him saying, 'Go away!' Disheartened, the beggar hobbled away and sat down in one corner of the temple, crying.

Satyavan felt sorry for the beggar. He left the line and went up to him. There was no food stall around the temple so he gave the beggar the milk that he had bought to offer to Lord Shiva. The hungry beggar began to drink up the milk.

Satyavan now couldn't go back to the line for the *darshan*. Though he badly needed the blessings of the Lord, he thought he would have to go without them. He knew his mother wouldn't be happy with him. Her anger could be managed. However, he hoped that God wouldn't be angry with him. But the beggar's words allayed all his fears on that subject.

Think Tank

1. What did the beggar say?

2. What is the implication of this story?

The Think Tank encourages you to answer these questions on your own before referring to the answers given below.

Answers

1. The beggar said, 'God bless you, my child!'

2. One hand offering help to someone is worth more than two hands joined in prayer.

JAICO PUBLISHING HOUSE
Elevate Your Life. Transform Your World.

ESTABLISHED IN 1946, Jaico Publishing House is home to world-transforming authors such as Sri Sri Paramahansa Yogananda, Osho, The Dalai Lama, Sri Sri Ravi Shankar, Sadhguru, Robin Sharma, Deepak Chopra, Jack Canfield, Eknath Easwaran, Devdutt Pattanaik, Khushwant Singh, John Maxwell, Brian Tracy and Stephen Hawking.

Our late founder Mr. Jaman Shah first established Jaico as a book distribution company. Sensing that independence was around the corner, he aptly named his company Jaico ('Jai' means victory in Hindi). In order to service the significant demand for affordable books in a developing nation, Mr. Shah initiated Jaico's own publications. Jaico was India's first publisher of paperback books in the English language.

While self-help, religion and philosophy, mind/body/spirit, and business titles form the cornerstone of our non-fiction list, we publish an exciting range of travel, current affairs, biography, and popular science books as well. Our renewed focus on popular fiction is evident in our new titles by a host of fresh young talent from India and abroad. Jaico's recently established Translations Division translates selected English content into nine regional languages.

Jaico's Higher Education Division (HED) is recognized for its student-friendly textbooks in Business Management and Engineering which are in use countrywide.

In addition to being a publisher and distributor of its own titles, Jaico is a major national distributor of books of leading international and Indian publishers. With its headquarters in Mumbai, Jaico has branches and sales offices in Ahmedabad, Bangalore, Bhopal, Bhubaneswar, Chennai, Delhi, Hyderabad, Kolkata and Lucknow.

SINCE 1946